THE SOUTHWE

A PICTORIAL HISTORY OF THE LAND AND ITS

BY STEVEN L. WALKER

Above: "Inscription Rock," El Morro National Monument, New Mexico. This 200 foot-high sandstone monolith has been a landmark for travelers for more than 700 years. The Anasazi inhabited the area from around A.D. 1275 until about 1350, leaving petroglyphs on the rocks. Early Spanish explorers, led by Juan de Oñate in 1605, left inscriptions on the rock, as did a succession of Anglo-Americans beginning with U.S. Army cartographer Lt. J. H. Simpson and artist R.H. Kern on September 17, 1849.
PHOTO BY TOM BEAN

Front Cover: Sunrise captures the textures and colors of eroded sandstone and petrified sand formations at Paria Canyon, Vermilion Cliffs Wilderness. Southwestern artists, from early Paleo-Indian rock painters to contemporary artists, have long been inspired by the region's colors and textures.
PHOTO BY JACK W. DYKINGA

Left: White House Ruin, an Anasazi culture cliff dwelling in Canyon de Chelly, was abandoned by the Anasazi around A.D. 1300.
PHOTO BY TOM DANIELSEN

Above: Autumn frames the Great White Throne in Zion National Park, Utah.
PHOTO BY JEFF GNASS

Designed by Camelback Design Group, Inc., 8655 East Via de Ventura, Suite G200, Scottsdale, Arizona 85258. Phone: 602-948-4233. Distributed by Canyonlands Publications, 4860 North Ken Morey Drive, Bellemont, Arizona 86015. For ordering information please call (520) 779-3888.

Requests for additional information should be made to: Camelback/Canyonlands Venture at the address above, or call our toll free telephone number: 1-800-283-1983.

Library of Congress Catalog Number: 93-072734
International Standard Book Number: 1-879924-09-9

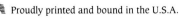 Proudly printed and bound in the U.S.A.

INTRODUCTION

The earliest inhabitants of the Southwest migrated from Asia via an ancient land bridge across the Bering Strait during the Pleistocene Epoch, or Ice Age, at least 37,000 years ago. The exposed land allowed grazing animals and early hunters access to the New World in migrations that lasted until the end of the Ice Age, around 11,000 years ago.

These early hunters were true men, walked erect, possessed fire, wore clothing of fur and skin, and used tools made of flint and bone. They were replaced, or assimilated, by Paleo-Indian groups that culminated in three major Southwestern prehistoric Indian cultures: the Hohokam, Mogollon and Anasazi.

The Hohokam were desert farmers who lived in villages in the Sonoran Desert for more than a millennia. They were the first Southwestern farmers to use irrigation, digging canals along the Gila and Salt Rivers. The Mogollon were primarily hunters and gatherers in mountain regions of southeast Arizona and southwest New Mexico. The Anasazi culture appeared around the birth of Christ in the Four Corners region of the Colorado Plateau. The Anasazi are best known for the cliff dwellings they inhabited during later years of their civilization.

In addition to the three major cultures, two minor cultures played a significant role in the prehistory of the Southwest. The Sinagua were farmers who inhabited the area around the San Francisco Peaks beginning about A.D. 500. The Salado culture, named for the Salt River (Rio Salado in Spanish) that was central to their way of life, inhabited the Tonto Basin for a short period between A.D. 1150 and 1450.

Exploration of the Southwest by Spanish explorers began without auspicious results. The first explorers through the region found it of little economic interest and were unsuccessful in fulfilling their goal of adding wealth to the Spanish crown. The Franciscan and Jesuit missionaries were responsible for much of the Spanish colonization of the region, although they met with much resistance from the Native Americans, who had little use for a new God.

The Spaniards failed to gain a significant foothold in the Southwest. Uneasy relations with the Indians kept them contained to small areas, and even then continual raiding by hostile Indians tribes was not conducive to the growth of their settlements.

In the early 1800's, Mexican Independence from Spain resulted in a change in control of much of the Southwest to Mexican hands. By 1835, the Texans gained their hard won independence from Mexico, with Mexican rule being replaced by the Americans throughout the territory by 1847.

The Americans entered the Southwest after the Mexican War and were successful in subduing the Native American inhabitants. Superior weaponry and forces were brought against the last raiding bands of Comanches, Apaches, Utes, Navajos and other tribes that had successfully resisted Spanish colonization.

Southwestern Indians of historic times are related in part to the prehistoric Pueblo cultures, Plains Indians, and Athabascan nomadic tribes from Canada. Today, Indians of the Southwest are known worldwide for their quality arts and crafts, and for their colorful traditions.

Preceding Pages: Sunrise along the South Rim of the Grand Canyon. Spanish explorers first learned of the Grand Canyon from the Hopi Indians on Coronado's expedition of 1540.
PHOTO BY CARR CLIFTON

Left: "Organ Pipes" rock formation at Chiricahua National Monument in southeastern Arizona. The Chiricahua Apache called this area the "Land of Standing-Up Rocks."
PHOTO BY DICK DIETRICH

Right: San Xavier del Bac, Tucson, Arizona. Called the "White Dove of the Desert," this centuries old Mission is one of the best examples of Spanish colonial architecture found in the Southwest.
PHOTO BY DICK DIETRICH

GEOGRAPHY OF THE SOUTHWEST...

The Southwest has no distinct boundaries. It is a land bound together by similarities in geography and by the cultures of its inhabitants, both prehistoric and historic. Most scholars agree that the region includes the states of New Mexico and Arizona, the southern portions of Utah and Colorado, southern and western Texas, and the northern reaches of Mexico.

The western boundary of the Southwest is normally defined by the Colorado River, although lands to the west of the river, in California and southern Nevada, share much in common with those of the western desert areas of Arizona. In the east, the Southwest merges with the Plains, once again defying a sharp breaking point, but generally including lands to the west and south of the Colorado Rocky Mountains. The plains of the Llano Estacado in eastern New Mexico and western Texas lend no help in clearly defining an eastern boundary. To the south, the International Border between the United States and Mexico forms an artificial line of demarcation as lands to both sides of the border, either in Arizona, New Mexico and Texas or in Mexico, show no physiographic differences.

The Southwest may be culturally defined as the region to the north of the Mesoamerican civilizations, to the south of the Great Basin and Rocky Mountains cultures, east of the Pacific Coastal cultures and west of the Plains cultures. These neighboring cultural areas share similar customs, and have long enjoyed trade relations with the Southwestern cultures.

The people of the Southwest share a common history; prehistoric cultures shared similar traits and interacted through trade. Everyone in the region was affected by the Spanish exploration and colonization, Mexican American War, and the Indian uprisings of the 1800's.

PARKS AND MONUMENTS OF THE SOUTHWEST

The Southwest is rich in recreational, scenic, cultural and historic sites that are preserved and operated by the National Park Service and by individual state and local governments.

Arizona has 22 sites under management by the National Park Service and 18 state parks. Colorado has 38 state parks and eleven sites that are run by the National Park Service. New Mexico has thirteen National Park Service sites and 37 state park and recreation areas. The state of Texas, with thirteen National Park Service sites, operates 105 state parks and recreation areas. Utah, with five national parks, a national historic site, six national monuments and two national recreation areas, has 45 state parks.

In addition to National Park Service and state park facilities, the Southwest has tens of millions of acres of U.S. Forest Service and BLM land that are available for outdoor recreation. The region contains an abundance of museums, zoos, historic sites and natural areas that offer a wealth of activities for visitors.

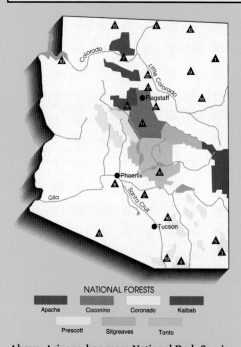

NATIONAL FORESTS

Apache · Coconino · Coronado · Kaibab
Prescott · Sitgreaves · Tonto

Above: Arizona has more National Park Service sites-with 22, than any other state in the U.S.

▲ Arizona's National Parks and Monuments

1 Canyon de Chelly National Monument
2 Casa Grande Ruins National Monument
3 Chiricahua National Monument
4 Coronado National Memorial
5 Fort Bowie National Historic Site
6 Glen Canyon National Recreation Area
7 Grand Canyon National Park
8 Hohokam Pima National Monument
9 Hubbell Trading Post National Historic Site
10 Lake Mead National Recreational Area
11 Montezuma Castle National Monument
12 Navajo National Monument
13 Organ Pipe Cactus National Monument
14 Petrified Forest National Park
15 Pipe Spring National Monument
16 Saguaro National Monument
17 Sunset Crater Volcano National Monument
18 Tonto National Monument
19 Tumacacori National Historical Park
20 Tuzigoot National Monument
21 Walnut Canyon National Monument
22 Wupatki National Monument

THE SEVEN LIFE ZONES

In the study of ecology, the science dealing with all living things, seven life zones have been established between the Equator and the North Pole. The study of life zones was formulated by Clinton Hart Merriam, one of the world's great naturalists, for the Department of Agriculture during the late 1800's and early 1900's.

Traveling through the Southwest, from the dry desert areas of Arizona along the Colorado River, to the towering mountain peaks of Arizona, Utah, Colorado and New Mexico, visitors pass through each of the seven life zones, the equivalent of a trip from the Equator to the North Pole. Merriam based his study on the premise that changes in elevation of 1,000 feet will have the same effect on plant life, and animal life, as a change of 300-500 miles in latitude. Merriam also determined that temperatures drop between 3-5 degrees for each 1,000 foot rise in elevation.

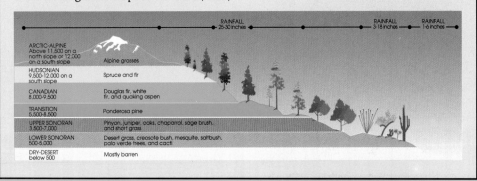

| RAINFALL 25-30 inches | | RAINFALL 3-18 inches | RAINFALL 1-6 inches |

ARCTIC-ALPINE Above 11,500 on a north slope or 12,000 on a south slope	Alpine grasses
HUDSONIAN 9,500-12,000 on a south slope	Spruce and fir
CANADIAN 8,000-9,500	Douglas fir, white fir, and quaking aspen
TRANSITION 5,500-8,500	Ponderosa pine
UPPER SONORAN 3,500-7,000	Pinyon, juniper, oaks, chaparral, sage brush, and short grass
LOWER SONORAN 500-5,000	Desert grass, creosote bush, mesquite, saltbush, palo verde trees, and cacti
DRY-DESERT below 500	Mostly barren

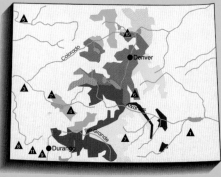

NATIONAL FORESTS

Arapaho · Grand Mesa · Gunnison · Pike
Rio Grande · Roosevelt · Routt · San Isabel
San Juan · Uncompahgre · White River

▲ Colorado's National Parks and Monuments

1 Bent's Old Fort National Historic Site
2 Black Canyon of the Gunnison Natl. Mon.
3 Colorado National Monument
4 Curecanti National Recreation Area
5 Dinosaur National Monument

NATIONAL PARKS AND MONUMENTS...

6   Florissant Fossil Beds National Monument
7   Great Sand Dunes National Monument
8   Hovenweep National Monument
9   Mesa Verde National Park
10 Rocky Mountain National Park
11 Yucca House National Monument

8   Golden Spike National Historic Site
9   Hovenweep National Monument
10 Mormon Pioneer Trail
11 Natural Bridges National Monument
12 Rainbow Bridge National Monument
13 Timpanogos Cave National Monument
14 Zion National Park

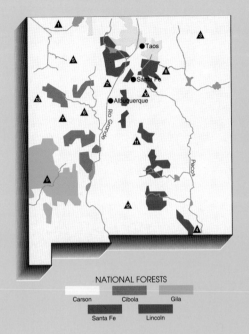

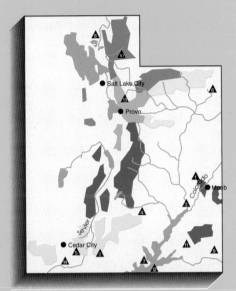

NATIONAL FORESTS

Carson   Cibola   Gila

Santa Fe   Lincoln

NATIONAL FORESTS

Angelina   Davy Crockett   Sam Houston   Sabine

NATIONAL FORESTS

Ashley   Dixie   Fishlake

Uinta   Wasatch-Cache   Manti-La Sal

▲ Utah's National Parks and Monuments

1   Arches National Park
2   Bryce Canyon National Park
3   Canyonlands National Park
4   Capitol Reef National Park
5   Cedar Breaks National Monument
6   Dinosaur National Monument
7   Glen Canyon National Recreation Area

▲ New Mexico's National Parks and Monuments

1   Aztec Ruins National Monument
2   Bandelier National Monument
3   Capulin Volcano National Monument
4   Carlsbad Caverns National Park
5   Chaco Culture National Historical Park
6   El Malpais National Monument
7   El Moro National Monument
8   Fort Union National Monument
9   Gila Cliff Dwellings National Monument
10 Pecos National Historical Park
11 Salinas Pueblo Missions National Mon.
12 White Sands National Monument
13 Zuni-Cibola National Historical Park

▲ Texas' National Parks and Monuments

1   Alibates Flint Quarries National Monument
2   Amistad National Recreation Area
3   Big Bend National Park
4   Big Thicket National Preserve
5   Chamizal National Memorial
6   Fort Davis National Historic Site
7   Guadalupe Mountains National Park
8   Lake Meredith National Recreation Area
9   Lyndon B. Johnson National Historical Park
10 Padre Island National Seashore
11 Palo Alto Battlefield National Historic Site
12 Rio Grande Wild and Scenic River
13 San Antonio Missions Natl. Historical Park

Right: Utah's Bryce Canyon National Park in winter, from Paria View.
PHOTO BY DICK DIETRICH

7

ANCIENT INHABITANTS

The first human inhabitants of the Southwest, and the New World, were the Texas Paleo-Americans, nomadic bands that roamed the region more than 37,000 years ago in pursuit of large prehistoric animals including mastodons, mammoths, camels and elephants. Surprisingly, these early hunters were not Asians but are thought to have been a Caucasoid race distinctly different from the later Paleo-Indians who wandered into the New World in pursuit of the now extinct prehistoric big game animals thousands of years later.

The earliest inhabitants of the Southwest were descendants of *Homo sapiens* who migrated from Asia via an ancient land bridge across the Bering Strait during the Pleistocene Epoch, or Ice Age, at least 37,000 years ago. At this time, nearly one-sixth of the world's surface was covered with ice; formation of massive glaciers caused the oceans to recede and in some places sea level was lowered by as much as 300 feet, exposing a 56 mile strip of the ocean's floor between northeastern Siberia and northwestern Alaska. The exposed land allowed grazing animals and early hunters access to the New World.

These early hunters were true men, walked erect, possessed fire, wore clothing of fur and skin, and used tools made of flint and bone. Their greatest concentrations of fire sites and artifacts have been found on the limestone plateaus of Texas, where the oldest remains of man in the New World have been discovered. Radiocarbon testing has proven that remains of burnt wood from one campsite found in the region date beyond the range of the carbon-14 technique, which can establish dates as far back as 37,000 years ago.

Archeologists named these early hunters the Texas Paleo-Americans and were surprised to discover that they had massive teeth, longer heads than any race of modern man, and leg bones that were flat and curved. They were quite unlike the later Paleo-Indians or prehistoric American Indians who were previously thought to have been the earliest inhabitants of the New World. It is thought they were a Caucasoid race that originated in Central Asia.

Like all people of the Ice Age, these ancient people pursued herds of elephants, mastodons, mammoths, giant sloths, camels, horses and prehistoric bison (approximately twice the size and perhaps four times the weight of those found in recorded history). It is believed they led their nomadic existence in the New World for several thousand years before disappearing from the archeological record. It is currently unknown whether their race died out entirely or was changed so much over the following millennia they were no longer recognizable. What is known is that the next Southwestern inhabitants discovered by archeologists, also big game hunters, were distinctly Asian and bore no resemblance to the earlier inhabitants.

The first of these early Asian nomadic tribes to reach the regions of the Southwest, more than 12,000 years ago, are known as the Big Game Hunters or the Elephant Hunters. These early nomads found the region quite different than it is today. Climactic conditions were far more tropical: a juniper savanna covered the arid desert surrounding Las Vegas, Nevada; an open savanna of pine and spruce, dotted with shallow lakes, filled the now treeless plains of the Llano Estacado in eastern New Mexico and Texas; and Late Pleistocene streams flowed throughout the Southwest. This environment provided habitat for mastodons, mammoths, elephants, horses, camels, antelope, bison, sloth, tapir, peccary, deer, and rabbit–and for hunters who preyed on them for survival.

Paleo-Indian hunters depended on hunting the larger prehistoric beasts. Using organized teamwork to kill their prey, these Paleo-Indian

Left: Montezuma Castle, erroneously named after the famous Aztec Chief, is a Late Stage dwelling of the Sinagua constructed in the thirteenth century.
PHOTO BY GEORGE H.H. HUEY

Right: "Lion" Petroglyph at Rinconada Canyon in Petroglyph National Monument, New Mexico. Indian artists painted, or carved, drawings on rock surfaces. Petrogylphs were made by scratching a design into a rock's surface. Drawings created by painting a rock's surface are called pictographs.
PHOTO BY TOM BEAN

hunters fashioned spearheads of stone with detachable foreshafts. When the shaft became detached after entering the prey, the animals could not easily work the embedded point from wounds, which hastened the animal's death.

The exact arrival of Paleo-Indian inhabitants in the region is still unknown. Conservative archeologists currently place the date between 10,000-12,000 B.C. Archeologists during this century have been able to establish ground work to support early man's presence in the region. In 1927, J. D. Figgins discovered man-made artifacts in association with extinct mammals at the Folsom site in New Mexico, that have been dated at around 9000 B.C. The Folsom site was discovered by a cowboy, George McJunkin, in the 1920's. In 1928, Byron C. Cummings uncovered a similar find at the Double Adobe site in southeastern Arizona.

Two kill sites, excavated by archeologists from the University of Arizona in the 1950's, were discovered in Arizona and have been dated approximately 11,000 years ago. In the first, along the banks of Greenbush Creek near Naco in southeastern Arizona, an extinct mammoth was excavated. Archeologists found eight stone spearheads in the skeletal remains of the body portion of the 13 foot-tall animal. A second site, along the San Pedro River on Lehner Ranch, unearthed the bones of nine elephants along with a primitive horse, a bison, and a tapir. Ashes from two fires in the vicinity, probably made to roast meat from the kill, have been carbon dated to place the event near 9000 B.C.

The early Big Game Hunters harvested most of their needs from the mammals they hunted. After a group of men would kill an animal, normally from ambush near a watering hole, women would use stone knives to strip the animal's hide from its carcass, using stone scrapers to remove fat and flesh, a process that helped preserve and shape the hide which was then fashioned into clothing, robes and other useful items.

Archeologists have developed many theories about earlier cultures based on the remnants of their tool kits. Refinements in design of projectile points, such as the first appearance of longitudinal grooves on both faces of a spearhead so blood would flow more freely from a wound, helps to distinguish one culture from another. Archeologists name projectile points for the location they are first discovered. Sandia, Clovis and Folsom points are named for New Mexico sites. A projectile point may first be discovered in one area, although it is never certain that particular area was its point of origin or if it was obtained through trade, captured in war, or acquired by other means.

As the polar ice caps melted, the Southwest's climate became increasingly drier between 8000 and 7000 B.C., causing a decrease in annual rainfall of three to four inches and an increase in mean annual temperature between three and four degrees. Lush vegetation the larger mammals depended on for survival became increasingly scarce, as did the animals themselves. Final extinction of mammoths, mastodons, camels, elephants, horses and other large species may have been hastened by the Big Game Hunters themselves as they struggled to find the last of the diminishing herds to support their bands. Consequently, the Big Game Hunters themselves disappeared.

It is uncertain whether the next inhabitants to appear, Paleo-Indians evidenced by discovery of complexes including the Clovis culture, dating earlier than 9000 B.C.; Folsom culture, slightly after 9000 B.C.; Agate Basin culture around 8000 B.C.; and Cody culture of about 6500 B.C., were descendants of the Big Game Hunters or new arrivals to the Southwest. Currently, a gap in the archeological record of around 500 years exists which makes it uncertain if the Big Game Hunters moved on to the Great Plains or other regions, developed into arid-land dwellers, or were replaced by an entirely new group of people. What is known is that these new arid-land dwellers were forced to rely on a more varied diet.

Clovis finds have been reported over the entire Southwest and much of the Great Basin. Folsom complexes have been found east of the Arizona-New Mexico border. Remains of the Agate Basin complex occur in central and eastern New Mexico and the Cody complex is widely spread over the eastern and northern Southwest. At present, there is no evidence of a direct relation between these cultures and the earlier Big Game Hunters.

Early Archaic cultures, often characterized as belonging to the widespread Desert Culture, include four distinct groups: the Western, or San Dieguito-Pinto, who inhabited western Arizona and southern Nevada; the Southern, or Cochise tradition, found in the southeastern and east-central regions of Arizona and New Mexico's southwestern and west-central areas;

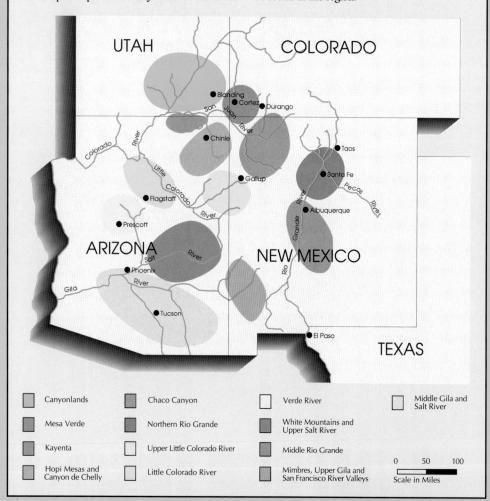

CONCENTRATIONS OF PREHISTORIC RUINS OF THE SOUTHWEST

The Southwest plays an important role in the preservation of artifacts of the New World's earliest inhabitants. The regions semi-arid climate has helped to preserve many artifacts that could not have survived in regions with a wetter climate. The map below shows areas with the greatest concentrations of aboriginal artifacts to be found in the region.

Legend:
- Canyonlands
- Mesa Verde
- Kayenta
- Hopi Mesas and Canyon de Chelly
- Chaco Canyon
- Northern Rio Grande
- Upper Little Colorado River
- Little Colorado River
- Verde River
- White Mountains and Upper Salt River
- Middle Rio Grande
- Mimbres, Upper Gila and San Francisco River Valleys
- Middle Gila and Salt River

0   50   100
Scale in Miles

the Northern, or Oshara tradition, of northern Arizona, southeastern Utah, southwestern Colorado, and northwestern New Mexico; and the Southeastern tradition, represented by Fresnal and Hueco related complexes.

The last areas of the Southwest abandoned by the Big Game Hunters of the Cody complex, around 6000 B.C., were the northeastern and southeastern regions. The San Dieguito-Pinto were then established in the west and the Cochise people were inhabiting the south. After environmental changes caused the last of the large mammal hunters to leave the region, the Oshara tradition began to appear.

Cultural remains of the San Dieguito-Pinto tradition, thought to date from approximately 7000 B.C. until sometime after 5000 B.C., closely resemble those of the earlier Clovis culture found to the east. Recovered tools, including a variety of scrapers, knives and projectile points, show them to have been unspecialized hunters and gatherers.

The Cochise culture, named for artifacts found along creek banks in Cochise County, Arizona, appeared at their earliest sites, called the Sulpher Springs phase, between 7000 B.C. and 6000 B.C. and were forced to adjust to an environment with fewer resources. A lack of the larger mammals resulted in the hunting of smaller animals and gathering of nuts, roots, grains, and berries to supplement their diets.

The Oshara tradition is representative of the northern Southwest between 5500 B.C. and A.D. 400. Early Archaic materials recovered belonging to the Oshara tradition date between 5500 and 4800 B.C. Tool kits and settlement

PROJECTILE POINTS

Prehistoric Indians of the Southwest all relied on some form of projectile point, or tip, to help penetrate their prey. A projectile point was affixed to the shaft of a spear in the earliest cultures. The atlatl, a rigid board around two feet long with a notch near the top in which the shaft

Projectile points found at Homolovi Ruins.
PHOTO BY MICHAEL COLLIER

of a spear, dart or arrow was inserted, was used from about 10,000 B.C. until the first centuries A.D. when it was replaced by the more accurate and powerful bow and arrow.

Projectile points are named for the location where they are first discovered and are used to aid in identifying different cultures by the refinements in design of the points, such as the appearance of longitudinal grooves to allow blood to flow freely from wounds. Prehistoric Southwestern projectile points have been found made of obsidian, rhyolite, jasper, calcite and other rocks and minerals.

patterns differ so greatly that no connection with the earlier Cody complex or other Paleo-Indians is clearly evident. Deer and bighorn sheep were the larger game animals and the people were now gatherers in addition to hunters. Seeds, berries, nuts, roots, and other plant parts were collected and small game such as rodents, rabbits, birds and squirrels were killed with spear and dart throwers, called atlatls, or trapped with snares. Even insects and reptiles became part of the people's diets.

Change to a diet that partly included plants necessitated new levels of resourcefulness and ingenuity. Seeds needed to be finely ground to be digested. Grinding stones were developed with the bottom stone hollowed out to contain the grain and the top stone shaped to fit the hand as it was rolled over seeds until they became reduced to a powder. Beaters, trays and baskets were made to collect, carry and store food. Waterproofing with resins and gums was introduced to store water and allow the cooking of grains into gruel and flat cakes. During this development stage, Southwestern cultures, still nomadic, wandered the region in pursuit of game and plant species.

The implementation of agriculture, perhaps as early as 3000 B.C., with plantings of corn, beans, squash and melons, set the stage for development of permanent villages. Crops were planted, using digging sticks to make holes in which seeds were placed, and then left to nature for water and nourishment as the planters continued to forage for plants and game. It was now necessary for the tribe to return to the area to harvest ripened crops, forming the basis for villages inhabited on a seasonal basis.

Even as agriculture played an increased role in the sustenance of Southwestern tribes, it was slow to change the way of life of those who domesticated the crops. Evidence of wells dug to provide water in dry areas has been found dating to this period near Clovis, New Mexico, and it is assumed they existed in other areas as well. Hunting and gathering were still essential for survival. It was not until around 300 B.C. that irrigation on a substantial scale appeared in villages along the Gila and Salt rivers, leading

MAJOR PREHISTORIC INDIAN CULTURES

The three major Indian cultures in the prehistoric Southwest were the Hohokam, who lived in river valleys in the southern desert and were an agricultural group; the Mogollon, who were hunter-gatherers; and the Anasazi, who were cliff dwellers. The Sinagua lived near Flagstaff and the Verde Valley and comprised traits from all three major cultures. The Salado lived in east-central Arizona and are thought to be a blend of two or more major cultures.

to an increased reliance on agriculture, as a major part of subsistence, and consequently paving the way for development of the first year-round villages.

Snaketown, on the north bank of the Gila River in Arizona, was a year-round village inhabited by the Hohokam from around 300 B.C. (although some put this date as late as A.D. 500) until A.D 1000. More than 200 rooms have been excavated and research has shown that Snaketown's inhabitants relied heavily on production of domesticated crops and had developed skillful irrigation techniques.

By A.D. 500, there were few permanently occupied Southwestern villages, as most tribes were still at least semi-nomadic, returning to base camps to plant and harvest crops while continuing to gather wild plant foods and hunt game to supplement their existence.

There were three major Indian cultures in the prehistoric Southwest: the Hohokam, a desert agricultural group; the Mogollon, hunters and gatherers in the mountain regions; and the Anasazi, cliff dwellers in later stages in northern areas of the Southwest. Other important groups included the Sinagua, who lived near Flagstaff and in the Verde Valley area, and the Salado, who lived in the Tonto Basin and mountains near Globe and Miami in east-central Arizona.

The Hohokam were noted for their irrigation systems, the largest in prehistoric North America, which brought tens of thousands of acres of the Sonoran Desert under cultivation through a series of gravity-fed canals, complete with dams and headgates. They also relied heavily on gathering wild plants including prickly pear, saguaro fruit and mesquite beans to supplement their fare.

In A.D. 1358, the Salt River rose to its highest level in 450 years and Hohokam fields and canals were abandoned for drier ground. After A.D. 1450, they disappeared from their villages. When the Spanish arrived, the Pima, probable descendants of the Hohokam, were living in the region.

The Hohokam, named from the Tohono O'odham/Pima word for "those who have vanished," or more accurately, "all used up," were desert farmers who lived in scattered villages in the Sonoran Desert of central and southern Arizona for more than a millennia. They were the first Southwestern farmers to use irrigation, digging gravity-fed canals along the Gila and Salt rivers. More than 300 miles of canals have been discovered in the Salt River Valley alone that were built by the Hohokam, the largest prehistoric system in North America.

Irrigation enabled the Hohokam to raise corn (maize), beans, barley, cotton, tobacco, squash, agave and more, allowing them to devote less time to foraging, although they did harvest pads of prickly pear cactus, saguaro fruit and mesquite beans to supplement their fare. This agricultural existence resulted in settlements and permanent villages located near the crops.

The Hohokam produced excellent pottery and clay figurines. Their stone tools, vessels, and art objects were also well made, as was their work with shells, mostly from the Gulf of California, which they used to fashion ornaments and mosaics of exceptional beauty. Designs were drawn on the shell with pitch; the shell was then soaked in an acidic solution–probably juice fermented from saguaro cactus fruit; the unprotected shell surface was etched by the acid, leaving the pitch-protected design raised. This process preceded European metal etching, developed during medieval times, by hundreds of years. Hohokam shellwork has been found at Anasazi, Mogollon, and Sinagua sites, most probably acquired by trade.

Some scholars place the Hohokam's arrival in the region at around 300 B.C. while others believe their arrival could be as late as A.D. 500. Debate over their origins also exists, with some archeologists believing they migrated from Mexico and others feeling the Hohokam and the Mogollon were descendants of the Cochise people. Most do agree to four major periods of Hohokam culture: Pioneer period–300 B.C. to A.D. 550 (some believe A.D. 300-500 is a more accurate arrival); Colonial period–A.D. 550 to 900; Sedentary period–A.D. 900 to 1100; and Classic period–A.D. 1100 to 1450.

During the Pioneer period the Hohokam lived in houses built in pits in the ground of mud and stick enclosed with clay. During the Colonial period true pithouses appeared with upright poles supporting roofs of reeds, grass and mud built over the pit. Increased trade and social interaction with Mexico was evident. Mesoamerican style ball courts, possibly used for semi-sacred games or at least as a center of community activity, began to appear.

During the Classic period major changes in architecture appear. Walled villages with multi-story above-ground adobe buildings appeared along with platform mounds, filled with trash, earth and covered with plaster, whose exact uses are still unknown. The end of the Classic period, during the fifteenth century, marks the end of the Hohokam. Controversy exists between those who believe Tohono O'odham (Papago), Pima and other Southwestern groups are descendants of the Hohokam and those who believe they replaced the Hohokam who had moved completely out of the region.

Left: Organ Pipe Cactus National Monument in southern Arizona. The diverse plants and wildlife of the area were utilized by the Hohokam and the Tohono O'odam (Papago) who are thought to be their descendants.
PHOTO BY BOB CLEMENZ

Right: Casa Grande Ruins National Monument. The first European to visit Casa Grande was a Jesuit missionary, Father Eusebio Francisco Kino, in 1694. The tower served as a landmark for early Spanish travelers. The four story tower is the largest existing Hohokam structure. The function of the tower has never been determined, although it may have been an astronomical observatory. In 1932, the National Park Service built the roof over the ruin to prevent its further erosion.
PHOTO BY GEORGE H.H. HUEY

THE MOGOLLON

The early Mogollon lived in small villages that were built on mountain ridges and high mesas. Pithouses were round or irregular in shape, built partially underground with wooden beams to support the roof structure, and were entered either down a ramp or a step. A large communal room, around 300 to more than 1,000 square feet, was a central part of village life. Lack of everyday items, or burial remains beneath the floors, suggests they were used for special purposes. From about A.D. 600 to 900, Mogollon pithouses were mostly rectangular and were more carefully constructed than earlier structures. During this period, the Mogollon moved from their earlier high ground into valleys closer to their fields. After A.D. 900, the Mogollon began to construct above ground dwellings of masonry construction.

The Mogollon were primarily hunters and gatherers in the mountain regions of southeastern Arizona and southwestern New Mexico. Their culture was named for the Mogollon Mountains of New Mexico by early archeologists who did not want to link their culture with living Native American groups. Although many Mogollon sites were excavated prior to 1920, archeologists of the time thought them to have been regional variations of the Anasazi (Hisatsinom) culture. By the first Pecos Conference in 1927, archeologists had begun to recognize several cultures in the Southwest instead of one culture with regional variations. In the early 1930's, H.S. Gladwin and Emil W. Haury were the first archeologists to recognize the Mogollon as a culture distinct from the Hohokam of southern Arizona deserts and the Anasazi of the Colorado Plateau to the north.

The Mogollon are now generally considered descendants of the earlier Cochise culture, whose earliest presence in the region dates to around 6000-5000 B.C. The Mogollon culture began to appear around 300-200 B.C. and, like their Cochise ancestors, settled in areas where animals they hunted, including deer, bison, pronghorn, rabbit, turkey and mountain sheep, were plentiful. The Cochise people were the first Southwestern culture to cultivate corn, and are thought to have passed this skill along to the Mogollon, who also grew small amounts of beans and squash, although they relied less on agriculture and more on hunting and gathering wild foods, than the neighboring Hohokam or Anasazi cultures. The Mogollon gathered wild foods including walnuts, prickly pear cactus, acorns, pinyon nuts, agave, tansy mustard, sunflower seeds and wild tomato. Agriculture became a more important source of sustenance for the Mogollon around A.D. 700, as they began planting improved strains of corn along with squash, beans and cotton.

The Mogollon were among the first Indian cultures of the Southwest to make pottery for storing food and water. Their earliest examples were a plain brown ware, called Alma Plain, and a polished red ware called San Francisco Red that appeared around A.D. 200. A red-on-brown painted type, Mogollon Red-on-brown, appeared about A.D. 300. Around A.D. 750, the Mogollon potters introduced a painted red-on-white ware called Three Circle Red-on-white, which marked a startling change in design and was popular and widely produced until about A.D. 900, when the red-on-brown and the red-on-white were completely replaced by black-on-white types that are thought to have been inspired by Anasazi designs. The black-on-white styles evolved into the Mimbres Classic Black-on-white wares the Mogollon produced until about A.D. 1200 and have since become famous for. The popularity and value of these wares, when first discovered, caused widespread looting of Mogollon ruins that devastated many important archeological sites.

The early Mogollon lived in small villages, normally less than fifty dwellings, that were built on mountain ridges and high mesas. The buildings were of pithouse construction, round or irregular in shape, partially underground with wood beams supporting the roof structure, and were entered either down a ramp or a step

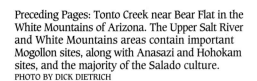

Preceding Pages: Tonto Creek near Bear Flat in the White Mountains of Arizona. The Upper Salt River and White Mountains areas contain important Mogollon sites, along with Anasazi and Hohokam sites, and the majority of the Salado culture.
PHOTO BY DICK DIETRICH

Left: Roof detail of Mogollon culture cliff dwellings in Gila Cliff Dwellings National Monument. The structures were built around A.D. 1270 and were abandoned by the early 1300's.
PHOTO BY GEORGE H.H. HUEY

Right: Kinishba Pueblo, west of Whiteriver, Arizona, contains the remains of two large structures of about 200 rooms each. Kinishba was occupied from around A.D. 1250 to 1325.
PHOTO BY MICHAEL COLLIER

that normally faced east or southeast. A large communal room, ranging from around 300 to more than 1,000 square feet, was a central part of village life. Lack of everyday living items, or burial remains of the dead beneath the floors, in excavations of these communal rooms suggest that they were used for special purposes. Although it cannot be said for certain they were for ceremonial uses, some contained artifacts that may point to religious usages.

From A.D. 600 to 900, Mogollon pithouses were mostly rectangular and more carefully constructed than earlier structures. During this period, the Mogollon moved from their earlier high ground into valleys that placed them closer to their fields. Anasazi influences began to show in their pottery and architecture.

About A.D. 900, the Mogollon began building their first surface pueblos. These structures were above ground and were of stone masonry construction. They ranged from 4 or 5 rooms to the 500 room Grasshopper Pueblo in the White Mountains of Arizona that was built between A.D. 1275 and 1300.

The Mogollon are not thought to have been a particularly inventive people. Most tools that have been uncovered at their ruins tend to be quite primitive. Many archeologists feel that advances in architecture and ceramic pottery by the Mogollon around A.D. 1000 were the result of the Anasazi moving into Mogollon areas and the only true Mogollon were the earlier pithouse builders. Others feel there was contact between the two cultures, and that the Anasazi influenced the Mogollon, but did not entirely replace them.

Mogollon sites from earlier periods are poorly preserved. Later developments, including the Gila Cliff Dwellings in New Mexico and the Kinishba Pueblo, with two large structures each with about 200 rooms, in the White Mountains of Arizona, are among the best preserved of Mogollon sites. Kinishba was occupied around A.D. 1250 to 1325 and contains traces of the Mogollon and Anasazi cultures.

Gila Cliff Dwellings National Monument also shows elements of both Mogollon and Anasazi cultures. About A.D. 1270, the Mogollon moved to the cliffs above Cliff Dweller Canyon, for reasons that are currently not completely understood but possibly include: a depletion of natural resources near, or overpopulation of, their former homelands; increased raiding by other Indian groups; or possibly infighting among themselves. At Gila Cliff Dwellings the Mogollon built masonry structures in a series of caves, high above the canyon floor, some of which are connected. These dwellings were occupied for only a short period of time and abandoned by the early 1300's. Although no one is exactly sure of the reasons they were abandoned, it may be that the Anasazi had completely absorbed this Mogollon group and they then may have left the area in search of more fertile farmlands.

One of the last pueblos to be occupied by the Mogollon was near Springerville, Arizona. Casa Malpais is a Spanish name meaning the "Badlands House." This 60-80 room pueblo was inhabited around A.D. 1265 to 1400. In 1990, archeologist John Hohmann examined Casa Malpais and discovered that fissures found in the caves, previously thought to have contained only trash, had been altered by their earlier inhabitants and contained about 3 to 4 acres of tunnels and chambers, some as wide as 50 feet and as much as 100 feet long.

These underground chambers were filled with human skeletal remains, unlike any site ever discovered north of Mexico. The State of Arizona gives some control over these remains to their likely descendants, in this case the Hopi and Zuni, who now control access to these underground catacombs. No burial remains or burial objects are allowed to be removed from the site, nor will photography be allowed. This unique discovery will undoubtedly change much of what archeologists currently believe about the ceremonial aspects of the Mogollon.

Although Mogollon abandonment of their homelands by A.D. 1400 is still somewhat of a mystery, there are several theories regarding their dispersal. Below average rainfall may have affected their crops, warring factions may have entered the region, or they may have been completely absorbed by the Anasazi who then left in search of better farmlands. Some believe they moved north into Zuni and Hopi country, which is a likely theory and is supported by both the Hopi and Zuni who claim the Mogollon as ancestors. Others believe they migrated to the Sierra Madre Mountains of Mexico where they became the Tarahumara Indians. It is probable that either one, or both, of these theories may be correct.

EVOLUTION OF MOGOLLON POTTERY...

The Mogollon were among the first Southwest Indian cultures to make pottery for storing food and water. Utilization of pottery for cooking allowed a more diverse and palatable fare than those previously cooked by placing heated stones and food together in baskets.

The earliest Mogollon pottery examples were a plain brown ware, known as Alma Plain, and a red ware called San Francisco Red that appeared around A.D. 200. Both styles were polished and unpainted. These plain wares were mainly jars and bowls that were continually produced throughout the entire Mogollon history.

Around A.D. 300 the painted Mogollon Red-on-brown ware began to appear, with broad red lines painted on a brown ware. After A.D. 750 Mogollon wares underwent a startling change to painted red-on-white wares known as Three Circle Red-on-white, which remained popular and were produced until about A.D. 900, when the red-on-white and the red-on-brown styles were completely replaced by black-on-white wares that are thought to have been inspired by Anasazi designs. With the introduction of the black-on-white wares, the Mogollon also added more shapes, styles and designs. Jars and bowls were joined by ladles, pitchers, and other vessels of various shapes and usages. These black-and-white wares evolved into the Mimbres Bold Face and Mimbres Classic Black-on-white styles that were produced by the Mogollon until about A.D. 1200. These bold designs are known for their geometric styles which depict animals, insects, birds, fish, and people, and include some very

Both Mimbres Bold Face and Mimbres Classic Black-on-white pottery were crafted by the Mogollon from A.D. 900 to 1200 and are some the finest examples of prehistoric pottery found in the Southwest. The holes in these items denote burial finds.
PHOTO BY JERRY JACKA

interesting combinations of different creatures that are combined into one stylized element.

Around A.D. 1100, polychrome pottery styles were developed by the Mogollon that included black and white designs painted on a red slipped background that were exquisite and are thought to have been produced mainly by the Mogollon, although at least some of these wares may have been trade items produced by other groups.

Of all Mogollon pottery, Mimbres Bold Face and Mimbres Black-on-white are considered to have been their crowning achievements. These pottery styles were so valued when they were first discovered that widespread looting of ruins to obtain the pottery by pothunters devastated many important Mogollon archeological sites.

Right: The more than forty cliff dwelling rooms at Gila Cliff Dwellings National Monument were built of stone and adobe mortar by the Mogollon around A.D. 1270. These structures were sheltered in six caves, about 175 feet above the canyon floor, some of which are interconnected.
PHOTO BY GEORGE H. H. HUEY

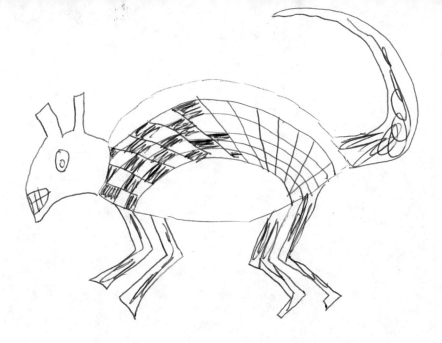

THE ANASAZI

The Anasazi (Hisatsinom) first appeared around the birth of Christ in the four corners region of the Colorado Plateau. Thought to have been descendants of a branch of an Archaic Desert Culture who inhabited the Southwest from approximately 6000 B.C., or a branch of the Mogollon who wandered into the region from the south, the Anasazi are best known for the cliff dwellings they inhabited during later years of their civilization. The ruins at Chaco Culture National Historical Park, Mesa Verde National Park and Canyon de Chelly National Monument, in addition to countless other sites scattered throughout the Colorado Plateau, are among the best preserved ruins found in North America and have attracted attention from around the world since their discovery in the late 1800's.

For the first 1,000 years of their civilization, however, the Anasazi did not construct the cliff dwellings they later became famous for; they lived instead in unprotected open-country communities. Their earlier dwellings, called pithouses, were structures built three to five feet in the ground with roofs supported by wooden poles and beams that were covered by brush and mud. The early Anasazi lived in small communities near the fields where they grew corn, squash and beans. They gathered wild foods including agave, walnuts, pinyon nuts, acorns, yucca, prickly pear, Indian ricegrass, and wild potatoes; gathered other plants for use as medicines, fuel and building materials; and hunted game such as elk, deer, pronghorn antelope, mountain sheep, rabbit, turkey, birds, fish and rodents. Archeologists believe, based on

this pattern of living in open country without the protection afforded by later cliff dwellings, that the Anasazi had relatively few, or perhaps no, natural enemies during these early years.

The various periods of the Anasazi culture have been defined by scientists as Basketmaker I, Basketmaker II, Basketmaker III, Pueblo I, Pueblo II, Pueblo III, Pueblo IV and Pueblo V. These earliest Anasazi (Hisatsinom) were the Basketmaker II and lived from about A.D. 1 to about A.D. 500. (The Basketmaker I designation is used for the earlier Archaic cultures believed by many archeologists to have been ancestors of the Anasazi.) Basketmaker II people grew crops of corn and squash, hunted with spears and spear throwers called atlatls and gathered wild foods which they stored in baskets. At this stage, the Anasazi had not developed pottery, so tightly woven baskets, some which were water proofed on the inside with a coating of pitch, and small woven bags were used for storage. They lived in caves, rock shelters and in some areas built circular log houses with slightly depressed floors.

The Basketmaker III period, from around A.D. 500 to A.D. 700, brought about a period of major change to the Anasazi. Pottery was developed which proved much more practical for storing water and cooking hot foods; beans, which provided a good source of protein, were added to the Anasazi crops; the more accurate bow and arrow replaced the spear and atlatl; and the people began to construct pithouses. These innovations added stability to Anasazi life, although gathering wild plants remained an important part of everyday life. The use of

Left: Giant patina draperies stain the overhang of the cave sheltering White House Ruins at Canyon de Chelly National Monument. The streaks, called desert varnish, are created as iron and manganese oxides stain the rock's surface.
PHOTO BY DICK DIETRICH

Right: Betatakin, a Navajo word meaning "ledge house," is a Kayenta Anasazi ruin protected in an alcove measuring 452 feet high, 370 feet wide and 135 feet deep. Although Betatakin, Keet Seel and Inscription House ruins are located on the Navajo Reservation at Navajo National Monument, the Navajo are not Anasazi descendants and entered the region long after the Anasazi moved south.
PHOTO BY LARRY ULRICH

pottery allowed better storage of surplus food stuffs for future use and so the Anasazi became less vulnerable to climactic cycles.

The Pueblo I stage began around A.D. 700 and lasted until A.D. 900. Toward the end of this period, pithouses were beginning to be replaced by above ground dwellings. Painted pottery emerged, although plainware was still predominant, with black-on-white, red-on-orange and black-on-red types appearing, and there is some evidence that agriculture increased in importance and sophistication.

During Pueblo II, from A.D. 900 to 1100, pottery designs became bolder and kivas, communal rooms used for special purposes, began appearing in most villages. During this stage, population appears to have significantly increased as numerous small villages appeared over a wide range.

The Pueblo III stage, from A.D. 1100 to 1300, found the Anasazi building larger and larger masonry villages, some several stories tall, frequently in caves and on mesa tops that were easily defensible, suggesting a new threat from outside forces thought to have been nomadic groups that were ancestors to the Utes and Paiutes. Pottery, jewelry and basket making was refined and trade with the neighboring cultures intensified. It is at the end of Pueblo III, however, that for reasons that are not completely understood, western

Anasazi sites, including the entire San Juan area, were largely abandoned and the eastern Anasazi sites experienced rapid expansion that lasted into the Pueblo IV stage.

The Pueblo IV stage, from A.D. 1300 until the arrival of the Spanish in 1598, found Anasazi in northern areas moving south to join the Hopis and Zunis. The existing eastern Anasazi pueblos continued to grow into larger settlements that often housed hundreds or thousands of people.

Of the many distinct Anasazi areas, Chaco in northwest New Mexico

Above: Perfect Kiva Ruin in Bullet Canyon, Grand Gulch Primitive Area near Blanding, Utah. In addition to the well-traveled Anasazi culture sites located throughout the Southwest, thousands more are accessible to serious students of prehistoric cultures who have proper transportation and permits.
PHOTO BY MICHAEL COLLIER

was the earliest to leave its Basketmaker III stage and to enter the Pueblo stages. Chaco Canyon was the center of Anasazi civilization by A.D. 900, and several great houses, roads, and irrigation systems had already been built. At its height, Chaco Canyon may have housed thousands of people, although most evidence points to a majority of occupation occurring on a seasonal basis, with a smaller year round

population. Three major building styles were developed: outlying villages of simpler styles thought to be homes for related family groups;

Below: Interior view of Cliff Palace at Mesa Verde National Park. Cliff Palace, with 217 rooms and 23 kivas, is the largest cliff dwelling in North America.
PHOTO BY GEORGE H. H. HUEY

Right: Cliff Palace at Mesa Verde National Park.
PHOTO BY GEORGE H. H. HUEY

THE ANASAZI CONTINUED...

Great Towns with huge room blocks that were carefully planned and built in coordinated stages with multiple levels up to 5 stories high; and Great Houses that also possessed large plazas, some with great kivas that also were carefully planned and constructed.

Chaco Anasazi were accomplished jewelry and ornament makers, producing exquisite turquoise items that are among the finest examples of Pueblo arts and crafts. Chaco Anasazi were actively involved with trade between other Anasazi groups and with other Southwest Indian cultures. Their population reached its height in the early A.D. 1100's and peaked around 1130. Twenty years later, following a long period of little precipitation, the Chaco people abandoned the region and moved to more hospitable areas.

Remains at Chaco Culture National Historic Park were first discovered by Americans in 1849, when Lt. James Simpson of the United States Army led a military action against the raiding Navajo in the area. Richard Wetherill, as leader of the Hyde Exploring Expedition from 1896 to 1900, was responsible for the

Left: Pueblo del Arroyo in Chaco Culture National Historical Park. The park's 18 square miles contain eighteen major ruins and countless smaller sites that may have housed up to 5,000 people.
PHOTO BY LARRY ULRICH

Below: Pecos Pueblo Ruin, an Anasazi pueblo that contained more than 650 rooms and 22 kivas in Pecos National Historical Park.
PHOTO BY GEORGE H. H. HUEY

earliest excavations at Chaco. In 1907, Chaco was designated as a national monument. In 1980, after the discovery of large outlying areas of significance, the national monument was expanded and redesignated as the Chaco Culture National Historical Park.

At Mesa Verde National Park, in southwestern Colorado, Anasazi Basketmaker III (Modified Basket Maker) pithouse remains dating between A.D. 575 and 800 have been discovered along with mesa top pueblo villages that began to be constructed around A.D. 800. Elaborate cliff dwellings were built during the thirteenth century in the shelter of caves. In all, the park contains more than 4,000 sites.

Mesa Top Ruins on Ruins Road Drive offers the chance to study early pithouse dwellings and pueblo villages with subterranean kivas. Sun Point Pueblo, dating around A.D. 1200, is the last of the mesa top developments and shows the first example of a kiva occupying the central plaza of a village. In the early 1200's, the residents of Sun Point Pueblo moved off the mesa top to cliff dwellings below, dismantling the village and using its stones and wooden timbers in construction of new homes. The tremendous

Above: Hovenweep Castle at Hovenweep National Monument. The largest structure at Square Tower Group, one of six groups of ruins within the National Monument, Hovenweep Castle has two towers, two kivas and numerous dwelling rooms.
PHOTO BY LARRY ULRICH

amount of labor involved in carrying stone and timbers along narrow paths into recesses in the cliff walls causes many to believe that a new threat to the Anasazi's security had

THE ANASAZI CONTINUED...

resulted in the development of defensible cliff dwellings during the final stage of Mesa Verde's development and occupation.

Beneath the mesa top rim, some of the best preserved cliff dwellings in North America are carefully preserved. Cliff Palace, the largest cliff dwelling in North America, contains 217 rooms and 23 kivas and is thought to have had a population of around 200-250 people. Long House, with around 150 rooms and 21 kivas, is the second largest ruin within Mesa Verde National Park. Of the park's nearly 600 cliff dwellings, 75 percent contain between one and five rooms. Spruce Tree House, which is visible from a terrace patio outside the park's excellent museum, contained about 114 rooms and eight kivas. Balcony House, a medium sized cliff dwelling 600 feet above the canyon floor has been tree-ring dated. The first timbers were cut in A.D. 1190 and the last cut in A.D. 1282, placing it as one of the last sites to be abandoned, as most cliff dwellings in Mesa Verde do not date beyond the late A.D. 1270's. Although reasons for Anasazi abandonment of Mesa Verde are uncertain, it is thought that a depletion of the natural resources in the area, climactic changes in the region along with a prolonged period of drought, and internal strife may have caused the Mesa Verde Anasazi to leave their homes. Many scientists today believe they moved south to join the Hopi in Arizona, and Zuni, Acoma, Santo Domingo, San Felipe and other Rio Grande Pueblos to the east in what is now the state of New Mexico.

On December 18, 1888, Richard Wetherill, a Colorado rancher who was riding across the mesa top with his brother-in-law, Charlie Mason, became the first white men to stumble upon the remains of Mesa Verde. Wetherill

and other parties explored Mesa Verde sites over the following eighteen years. In 1906, the area achieved national park status. In 1909, Jesse Fewkes of the Smithsonian Institution excavated and stabilized Cliff Palace. In 1978, the park was designated a World Heritage Site, recognizing Mesa Verde National Park's unique anthropological sites.

Ute Mountain Tribal Park, encompassing approximately 125,000 acres on the western and southern boundaries of Mesa Verde, has been set aside by the Ute Mountain Ute Tribe to preserve Anasazi and Ute sites, including Tree House and other cliff dwellings in Lion Canyon that were built around A.D. 1140. Ute Mountain tours are conducted by members of the tribe and reservations in advance are required.

Aztec Ruins, located to the southeast of Mesa Verde in the Animas River Valley, in the San Juan Basin of northern New Mexico, was built in the early 1100's and is believed to have been a community that was part of the greater Chaco culture to the south and possibly a gathering place for ceremonial functions and as well as a trading center. Aztec Ruins, misnamed by early pioneers who felt they were too sophisticated to have been built by Southwestern Indians and were probably work of the Aztecs of Mexico, show signs of both Chaco and Mesa Verde influences. The main

ruin is 360 feet by 275 feet and may have contained around 500 rooms. A great kiva, reconstructed by Earl Morris in 1934, is the largest example of its kind and offers visitors

Above: Horsecollar Ruin, the largest Anasazi site in Natural Bridges National Monument in southeastern Utah. Anasazi inhabited White and Armstrong canyons of Cedar Mesa from about A.D. 100 to 1300. Natural Bridges National Monument contains three spectacular natural bridges carved by streams millions of years ago.
PHOTO BY GEORGE H. H. HUEY

to Aztec Ruins National Monument a chance to experience a kiva much as it must have appeared centuries ago.

Hovenweep National Monument, containing six separate groups of ruins, is located in San Juan County, Utah, and Montezuma County, Colorado. The Square Tower and Cajon groups are in Utah, and the Holly Canyon, Hackberry

Canyon, Cutthroat Castle and Goodman Point groups are in Colorado. The structures at Hovenweep, a Ute Indian word that means "deserted valley," were built at canyon heads and next to springs, possibly because there are no cliffs in the area for building cliff dwellings. Multi-storied structures, some square, oval, circular, and others "D" shaped, were built by Anasazi who farmed the Cajon Mesa from around A.D. 900 to 1300, when its residents abandoned the area. It is believed they moved south to join with other migrating Anasazi.

Navajo National Monument, on the Navajo

Indian Reservation in northeastern Arizona, was home to the Kayenta Anasazi from about A.D. 1250 until around 1300. Even though the area was inhabited for only a short period, the cliff dwellings in the Tsegi Canyon area of Navajo National Monument are some of the largest found. Betatakin, a Navajo word for "ledge house," with more than 135 rooms, and Keet Seel, a Navajo word meaning "broken pottery," with more than 150 rooms and six kivas, were built into huge alcoves in remote Tsegi Canyon's cliffs, far from the Anasazi's fields. Inscription House, in Nitsin Canyon some thirty-five miles from the visitors' center, is a three-storied structure that contained around eighty rooms and one kiva. By A.D. 1300 the

Left: The north side of West Ruin in Aztec Ruins National Monument. Aztec Ruins, misnamed by early pioneers who believed they were probably the work of the Aztecs of Mexico, show signs of both Chaco and Mesa Verde influences.
PHOTO BY GEORGE H. H. HUEY

Above: A Kayenta Anasazi ruin in the shelter of a cave in Monument Valley Tribal Park is one of numerous sites on the Navajo Indian Reservation in northern Arizona.
PHOTO BY TOM TILL

Right: Puerco Pueblo in Petrified Forest National Park was inhabited by the Anasazi until around A.D. 1400 and contained more than 100 rooms. Agate House, a partially restored pueblo found in the park, was constructed with the petrified wood for which the national park is now famous.
PHOTO BY TOM TILL

Kayenta Anasazi had left these canyon areas and are thought to have moved to the Hopi Mesas. Rock art found in Betatakin shows the Hopi Fire Clan symbol, which tends to support Hopi claims to the area as an ancestral site.

In 1895, Richard Wetherill, the Colorado rancher who had discovered Mesa Verde in 1888, accompanied by his brother Al and brother-in-law Charlie Mason, was guided to the area containing the ruins of Keet Seel by a Navajo Indian guide. In March of 1909, Navajo National Monument was established by then President Howard Taft to protect the ruins of Keet Seel. Within months of the establishment of the national monument, ruins at Betatakin and Inscription House were discovered.

Canyon de Chelly National Monument is also located on the Navajo Reservation. Its sheer walls and eroded formations have been the home to the Anasazi, Hopi and the Navajo for around 2,000 years. The Anasazi inhabited the region until about A.D. 1300, when they abandoned the area. The Hopi Indians, thought to be descendants of the Anasazi, occupied Canyon de Chelly sporadically until A.D. 1700, when they were replaced by the Navajo who still inhabit the region.

More than 700 prehistoric sites are contained within Canyon de Chelly National Monument, which also includes Canyon del Muerto, or "canyon of the dead," which was named for

the prehistoric Indian burial remains that were discovered in 1882 by James Stevenson, who was leading an expedition in the area. The prehistoric sites include pithouse remains, pueblos, and cliff dwellings. The cliff dwellings were constructed between A.D. 1100 and A.D. 1300 and include White House Ruins, Antelope House, Mummy Cave Ruin, and numerous other sites. The years of Anasazi occupation reflect a more peaceful time in the canyon's history, when compared with the written history of the area since the white man's intervention in the early 1800's.

The Navajo, fiercely independent and highly aggressive people related to the Apache, began to occupy Canyon de Chelly around 1700. Their uneasy relationships with Europeans and many Indian neighbors, who were the victims of their raids for around 150 years, often drove the Navajo to take refuge from pursuers in Canyon de Chelly. In 1805, the Spanish, under the leadership of Lt. Colonel Antonio Narbona, engaged the Navajo in a day-long battle in Canyon del Muerto. The Navajos took shelter in a cave, since called Massacre Cave, near the top of the canyon as Spanish forces fired on them from the canyon rim above. When the slaughter ended, more than 100 Indians were dead. Narbona, in his report to the governor of Santa Fe, stated that 115 Navajo were killed, including 90 warriors, and 33 were taken prisoner. The loss of life to the Spanish troops was limited to a single soldier who fell from the cliff to the canyon below.

When the area passed from Spanish and then Mexican control, to the Americans in 1848, the Navajo once again found themselves at odds with the white man. Increased raiding by the Navajo caused white settlers to seek protection. In 1864, Colonel Christopher "Kit" Carson, famous mountain man and Indian scout, engaged the Navajo at Canyon de Chelly and brought the raiding to an end by marching more than 8,000 Navajo to Fort Sumner, New Mexico, where they remained until allowed to return to their homeland four years later.

Canyon de Chelly National Monument was established on April 1, 1931, and contains more than 130 square miles of land entirely owned by the Navajos, who jointly operate the park with the National Park Service.

Petrified Forest National Park, although best known for its large concentration of petrified logs, has hundreds of prehistoric Indian sites that range from the Desert Archaic culture to the Anasazi and date from around 1050 B.C. to A.D. 1400. Campsite remains of the Desert Archaic culture, pithouse dwelling ruins of the Basketmaker Anasazi and multi-room pueblos of the Pueblo Anasazi are all found within the park's confines. Puerco Pueblo, near the Puerco River, was inhabited by the Anasazi until about A.D. 1400 and contained more than 100 rooms. Agate House, a partially restored pueblo also found in the park, was constructed with the petrified wood the park is famous for. The Anasazi of the Petrified Forest did not leave the area until around A.D. 1400, a late date for the western Anasazi, at which time they are thought to have moved to the Hopi Mesas or to other pueblos to the east.

The Anasazi are known to have inhabited the Grand Canyon, although the area was primarily a Hakatayan culture area. There is

evidence of some Basketmaker II utilization of the canyon although the majority of Anasazi sites date between A.D. 1050 and 1150. Most Grand Canyon sites are one or two rooms, or are granaries, although there are larger villages both at the canyon bottom and on the rim. The Tusayan Ruin, west of Desert View on the South Rim, is a two-story "U" shaped pueblo of around 30 rooms and dates from A.D. 1170 to 1205. Walhalla Glades Ruin on the North Rim was occupied sometime after A.D. 1050, and Bright Angel Pueblo, with six rooms and a kiva at the bottom of the canyon near the Colorado River, was built in two phases between about A.D. 1050 and A.D. 1140.

The Anasazi occupied Zion National Park from about A.D. 500 until 1200. Although they built none of the large pueblos or cliff dwellings found in other areas, a small dwelling and several granaries have been uncovered. The northern areas of the park may have been occupied during this period by the Fremont culture, who lived in pithouses and surface dwellings similar to early Anasazi pueblos. There is little evidence of interaction between these two groups. The Anasazi abandoned the Zion area earlier than most of their northern territory for reasons that are unknown, but may include problems

with other Indian tribes in the area.

Canyonlands National Park in Southeastern Utah features Anasazi pueblos that were not as elaborate as those found in the four corners region but were multi-room structures and were sometimes sheltered in caves, such as Tower Ruin in The Needles. The Anasazi in Canyonlands reached the peak of their culture between A.D. 1000 and 1200. Here, as in Zion and other northern areas of Anasazi territory, Anasazi co-existed with the Fremont culture, a less sophisticated group who was found throughout the northern two-thirds of Utah and Colorado during Classic Pueblo times.

At Bandelier National Monument, on the Pajarito Plateau in northern New Mexico, the Anasazi established permanent communities around A.D. 500; evidence exists of earlier Paleo-Indian hunters and Archaic hunter and gatherer inhabitants. The Basketmaker Anasazi are thought to have entered the region during the first century A.D., living in pithouses, hunting game, gathering plants, and growing crops of corn, squash, melons and beans.

As the Anasazi communities at Chaco and Mesa Verde were reaching their zenith, the people at Bandelier were still part of a simpler time. Mud and grass shelters and single room block and mud homes were built in enclaves that seldom had more than twenty rooms. As the Anasazi began to leave their Chaco and Mesa Verde homelands, around A.D. 1300, new dwellings began to be built at Bandelier

Above: An Anasazi granary in Zion National Park.
PHOTO BY GEORGE H. H. HUEY

Left: Nankoweap Ruin, an Anasazi granary above the Colorado River in the Grand Canyon.
PHOTO BY TOM TILL

Right: Tyuonyi Pueblo Ruin at Bandelier National Monument contained around 400 rooms and featured a large central plaza.
PHOTO BY GEORGE H. H. HUEY

that were influenced by Chacoan and Mesa Verde architecture. The soft volcanic tuff of the canyon walls was utilized to build larger pueblos on the canyon bottom. Tyuonyi, a multi-storied pueblo from this period that contained around 400 rooms and a large central plaza, was built in the open, away from the sheltering cliffs.

Long House, named for its 800 foot length, was multi-storied and built with viga holes that anchored roof beams to the cliff surface for two or three rows of rooms that extended outward from the cliff. In all, several thousand sites have been identified within Bandelier National Monument's boundaries. The area was abandoned by the early 1500's, and it is thought its inhabitants moved to other pueblos in the Rio Grande Valley, probably the Cochiti and San Ildefonso pueblos.

Bandelier was named for adventurer Adolph Bandelier who discovered the Frijoles Canyon ruins in October of 1880 with a Cochiti guide named Juan Jose Montoya. In February of 1916, a presidential proclamation by President Wilson established Bandelier National Monument.

Pithouse remains in Pecos National Historical Park in north-central New Mexico establish Anasazi inhabitants in this area at least as early as A.D. 800. It is thought Anasazi from the northwest joined those living at Pecos in the early twelfth century and began to build multi-storied pueblos, the most powerful of which was Pecos.

When the Spanish conquistadors first arrived at Pecos in 1540, Pecos was a four to five story fortress that sheltered around 2,000 people. It was a major center of trade between the Pueblo Indians and the Plains Indians. Spanish missions were established at Pecos starting in 1598 to convert the Pueblos to Christianity.

The largest mission church was finished by Franciscan Father Andrés Juarez in 1625, the remains of which lay beneath the ruins of a church built in 1717. During the Pueblo Revolt in 1680, the missions were destroyed by the Pueblo Indians and the Spanish were driven south to El Paso, Texas. The Pecos people then reclaimed the area and built a kiva in the ruins of the living quarters of the church.

In 1692, the Spaniards regained control of New Mexico, and Pecos entered into a new era of problems. Comanche raids and European diseases decimated the population until there were only about 200 Pueblo Indians remaining at Pecos in 1786. By 1838 the population had dwindled to seventeen people, who then moved to Jemez Pueblo, forever abandoning the once powerful Pecos Pueblo. In 1965 Pecos became a national monument and in 1990 the area was established as Pecos National Historical Park.

THE SINAGUA

The Sinagua were farmers who inhabited the area around the San Francisco Peaks beginning about A.D. 500. They were named by scientist Dr. Harold S. Colton in the 1930's for the Spanish phrase *sin* "without" and *agua* "water." Dr. Colton believed the Sinagua were a distinct culture that was unrelated to the Hohokam, Anasazi and Mogollon; others feel they were a branch of the Mogollon, or a part of the Western Anasazi, or a minor culture combining traces of the Hohokam, Anasazi and Mogollon cultures. Located in an area overlapped by the Hohokam, Mogollon and Anasazi, the Sinagua were at least influenced heavily by these cultures.

It is important to note that although there still exists controversy among archeologists regarding the origins of the Sinagua, and to a much lesser extent their final disposition at the height of their culture, the Hopi Indians have no doubt that the Sinagua and Anasazi of the region are their ancestral peoples. The Anasazi name comes from the Navajo language and means "ancient people who are not us" or "ancient enemies." Anasazi is offensive to the Hopi who call their ancestors the Hisatsinom, which literally means "people of long ago." Currently, many sources are endeavoring to change the Anasazi name to the more accurate Hisatsinom in deference to the Hopi.

The Sinagua were involved in trade between Hohokam, Anasazi (Hisatsinom), Mogollon and other Southwestern cultures. Copper bells and parrots from Mexico, turquoise from New Mexico, shells from the Pacific coast and Gulf of California, Hohokam and Kayenta Anasazi pottery, and pipestone (red argillite) from the Prescott area have all been found in Sinagua sites. Sinagua trade products were probably salt mined near Camp Verde, ornaments fashioned from turquoise and pipestone or from shells, and woven cotton textiles. Sinagua pottery and baskets were generally considered rather plain, although the fragile nature of basketry leaves few well-preserved examples; they were probably not a major trade item.

In addition to the exchange of goods between the Sinagua and neighboring cultures, there also appears to be a great deal of social and technological interchange. Hohokam style ball courts have been found at several Sinagua sites including Wupatki and Winona Village; ceremonial kivas normally associated with the Anasazi are in evidence; Hohokam, Anasazi, and Mogollon architectural influence is found throughout Sinagua sites; and Anasazi pottery may have inspired several of the predominant styles of Sinagua painted pottery.

In addition to their role as merchants, the Sinagua were also resourceful farmers, growing crops of corn, beans, squash and cotton. They depended mainly on rainfall to water their crops, since they had few reliable water sources suitable for irrigation. Wild plants were also gathered including hackberry, mesquite beans, prickly-pear fruit, yucca, agave, walnuts and other food stuffs. Of the approximately 240 varieties of plants native to the region, possibly as many as half were used for fuel, medicines, basketry materials, matting, thatching and other purposes; they were more valuable to the Sinaguan culture than domesticated crops.

Left: Wukoki Pueblo, Wupatki National Monument. Wukoki is a three-story Sinagua structure that contained seven or eight rooms and is one of more than 2,600 prehistoric sites found within Wupatki National Monument.
PHOTO BY TOM TILL

Right: Montezuma Castle, erroneously named after the famous sixteenth-century Aztec Indian chief, is actually a five-story dwelling of the Sinagua, constructed in an alcove above Beaver Creek in the Verde Valley during the twelfth century.
PHOTO BY GEORGE H.H. HUEY

The Sinagua also used the bow and arrow to hunt small and large game animals including deer, rabbit, pronghorn antelope, beaver and elk. (Elk was found only in the more mountainous regions of the northern Sinagua.)

The Sinagua culture has been divided into two branches, the northern and the southern. The northern Sinagua occupied the area near Flagstaff and the San Francisco Peaks from about A.D. 500 until the early fourteenth century. They lived a peaceful existence in timber pithouses, growing crops, hunting game and gathering wild foods until disaster struck in 1064. A volcano, the remains of which is Sunset Crater, began a series of eruptions that destroyed all vegetation within a two-mile radius of the cone and covered more than 800 square miles of the surrounding area with volcanic ash and cinders. The resulting crater was four hundred feet deep.

With the eruption of the volcano, the Sinagua fled their homes. When they drifted back into the area several years later the soil had been made more suitable for farming by the volcanic ash, which served as a moisture-retaining mulch. The renewed soil moisture allowed the Sinagua to re-utilize the area and attracted other Indian groups including Hohokam, Anasazi (Hisatsinom), and Mogollon. These advanced cultures influenced the Sinagua, who absorbed their customs and skills. Masonry pueblos of the Anasazi style began replacing Sinagua pithouses, although construction of pithouses

continued. The Sinagua and the new arrivals appear to have blended peacefully.

With the new skills the Sinagua acquired, they built the 60-70 room Elden Pueblo near present-day Flagstaff, where they lived from around A.D. 1070 until sometime around A.D. 1275. Turkey Hill Pueblo, northeast of Flagstaff, is a masonry pueblo of more than 30 rooms occupied during this same time period.

Among the best preserved, and most extensive northern Sinagua ruins, are the multi-storied pueblos found thirty miles north of Flagstaff at Wupatki National Monument. Wupatki's 56 square mile area contains more than 2600 prehistoric sites, a majority of which are post-eruption, although pithouses have been excavated, covered by a layer of volcanic ash, that pre-date the eruption. Many of the later sites show influences of the Anasazi, Hohokam and Mogollon who moved into the area after Sunset Crater's eruption.

Wupatki National Monument contains thirteen excavated ruins of structures. Nalakihu, Hopi for "long house," has ten ground floor and several second story rooms at the base of the trail leading uphill to the Citadel Ruin, which

had around thirty rooms. Remains of pottery found at these neighboring sites suggests their inhabitants were of different cultures prior to their relocation into these structures.

Wukoki, two miles east of the Wupatki ruin, is a three story structure with seven or eight rooms. Lomaki, another pueblo located within the national monument, has been tree ring dated with the earliest timber cut in A.D. 1192, and the latest cutting dated at 1205. Absence of later cutting dates probably means this site was abandoned by A.D. 1225.

Wupatki National Monument's largest site is its namesake, Wupatki Pueblo. Wupatki, a Hopi word meaning "tall house," has more than 100 excavated rooms and several unique features including a Hohokam style ball court, the only example in the Southwest constructed of stone masonry, and a large amphitheater.

Excavation work at Wupatki has led to other important archeological evidence. The skeletal remains of 42 macaws were unearthed, which leads scientists to believe that these colorful birds, not just their feathers, were trade items from Mexico. Bowls of cotton, and cotton seed, were discovered in quantity along with weaving tools, which supports the theory that cotton was grown in the region and that woven cotton textiles were an important trade item.

Walnut Canyon National Monument, seven miles east of Flagstaff, was occupied by the northern Sinagua from about A.D. 1100 until around 1250. The cliff dwellings include the

Above: Walnut Canyon National Monument was created in 1915 to end looting of Walnut Canyon by pot hunters in the late 1800's and early 1900's.
PHOTO BY CHUCK PLACE

Left: Tuzigoot National Monument contains the remains of Tuzigoot Pueblo, a Sinagua site near Clarkdale, Arizona, with more than 100 rooms.
PHOTO BY TOM TILL

Right: Palatki Ruin, near Sedona, consists of stone structures occupied by the southern Sinagua from about A.D. 1150 until around 1250.
PHOTO BY MICHAEL COLLIER

remains of more than 300 rooms. There are also surface dwellings, constructed by the Sinagua on the mesa above the cliff dwellings, along with pithouse remains from an earlier culture. Walnut Canyon ruins were not widely known until the Atlantic & Pacific Railway reached northern Arizona in the 1880's. These ruins proved a popular tourist spot and looters, known as pot hunters, removed many of the artifacts valuable in helping archeologists better understand the Sinagua culture. In 1915, the pillaging was ended with the creation of Walnut Canyon National Monument.

The southern Sinagua appeared in the Verde Valley area around A.D. 700. The area's lower elevations offered a mild climate, long growing season and a steady water supply from the Verde River, which flowed year-round. Leading a peaceful existence, early southern Sinagua grew crops, gathered wild foods and hunted game while living in traditional pithouses. In the ninth century small pueblos appeared. During this period the Hohokam were also found in the area. Remnants of irrigation canals for watering their crops still remain.

Tree ring dating of beams found in the ruins at Palatki and Honanki, near Sedona, place the development of these cliff dwellings between A.D. 1130 and 1300. The northern Sinagua began to arrive in the Verde Valley area during the early fourteenth century after a long period of drought, when winds had eroded the top soil of farm lands in the north.

Tuzigoot National Monument, a stone pueblo of more than 100 rooms overlooking the Verde River near Clarkdale, has provided valuable insight into the Sinagua culture. More than 400 gravesites have been found, with nearly half of the bodies belonging to infants and children, many of which were simply scooped out of nearby trash mounds. High infant mortality may have been one reason the Sinagua abandoned the area in the 1400's.

Montezuma Castle National Monument is comprised of two distinct locations: Montezuma Castle, two five-story pueblos built into the cliffs above Beaver Creek in Verde Valley; and Montezuma Well, a limestone sink partly filled with water from an underground spring that flows at the rate of 1.5 million gallons a day.

The Montezuma Well area features an excavated pithouse, rooms inside the sink, and two pueblos located near the rim. Montezuma Castle's two ruins have walls of limestone blocks. The upper ruin has twenty rooms high in an alcove in the cliff walls and can only be reached by two narrow trails that would have been easy to defend. The lower ruin at the base of the cliff has forty-five rooms that could only be reached by climbing ladders.

Although the Sinagua appeared to be secure in their Verde Valley settlements, for unknown reasons they completely abandoned the area around A.D. 1425. Scientists speculate this disappearance may have been the result of drought, warfare, or possibly disease. It is also believed they moved to the northwest where they may have joined certain Hopi clans.

Above: Sunset Crater National Monument. In 1064, Sunset Crater began a series of eruptions that covered around 800 square miles of the surrounding region with cinders and ash. The volcano's cone rises more than 1,000 feet; the crater is 400 feet deep. The eruptions caused the northern Sinagua to flee their homes. PHOTO BY TOM BEAN

THE SALADO

Tonto Polychrome design

The Salado culture, named for the Salt River (Rio Salado in Spanish) that was central to their way of life, inhabited the Tonto Basin in central Arizona for a relatively short period between A.D. 1150 and around A.D. 1450. Considered a minor culture by most archeologists, their origins are still debated by many scientists. The first to identify the Salado as a separate culture was anthropologist Erich Schmidt, who studied Armer Ruin, the remains of a fourteenth century village exposed as Roosevelt Lake receded during a drought in 1925, as well as Togetzoge, a pueblo near Miami, Arizona, with around 120 rooms. The excavations at Togetzoge revealed new red-on-buff pottery styles Schmidt called Gila Polychrome, which he felt introduced a new culture.

In 1930, archeologist Harold Gladwin was the first to name this new culture. Gladwin felt the Salado sites represented a distinct and separate culture, although other archeologists including Emil W. Haury, Gladwin's associate at the Gila Pueblo Foundation in Globe, Arizona, believed the Salado were a combination of other cultures, in Haury's opinion the Mogollon and Anasazi. Others feel they were a Hohokam and Sinagua cultural mix; an outpost group from Mexico; or Hohokam who had moved into the region, as evidenced by many similarities between the two cultures.

By the appearance of the Salado culture, Southwestern cultures were so intermixed that it is hard to distinguish where one culture ended and another began, and whether this was a result of trade and exchange of ideas, or assimilation of one group by another.

The Salado, thought to have moved into the Tonto Basin from the upper Little Colorado River area sometime around A.D. 1150, lived in above ground pueblos that show Hohokam influence. Adobe mud was used as mortar in masonry construction, and platform mounds of earth and trash, normally associated with the Hohokam, are present at some Salado sites. Some believe the Hohokam were influenced by the Salado, who may have peacefully joined the Hohokam in the middle of the fourteenth century after abandoning their Tonto Basin homes.

The Salado hunted deer, pronghorn antelope, bighorn sheep and small game, gathered wild foods, and grew crops including corn, beans and squash. These crops were irrigated using canals that reveal a strong Hohokam influence.

Besh-Ba-Gowah, located near Globe, Arizona contained around 200 rooms and was occupied from A.D. 1225 to 1400. Gila Pueblo, located just a mile from Besh-Ba-Gowah on the opposite side of Pinal Creek, contained around 400 rooms. Togetzoge has around 120 rooms in a pueblo near Miami, Arizona. Near Roosevelt Lake, Tonto National Monument contains dwellings in two caves. The Upper Ruin has 40 rooms and is around 250 feet above the Lower Ruin, which has 19 rooms and is 350 feet above the valley.

The Salado abandoned their Southwestern homes in the mid 1400's and, as with other Indian cultures of the period, considerable debate exists as to their final disposition. Some archeologists believe they joined the Zuni, Hopi, or both, in their pueblos, while others feel they may have moved into northern Mexico.

Left: Lower Ruin at Tonto National Monument. The Lower Ruin has 19 rooms, the Lower Ruin Annex has an additional eleven rooms and the Upper Ruin has around 40 rooms.
PHOTO BY GEORGE H. H. HUEY

Right: Besh-Ba-Gowah Pueblo, Globe, Arizona. This Salado ruin contains around 200 rooms and was excavated and partially restored in the late 1930's by Irene Vickery.
PHOTO BY MICHAEL COLLIER

THE SPANISH INFLUENCE

The early Spanish explorers of the Southwest, Conquistadors and Franciscan missionaries, came in search of the legendary Seven Cities of Gold. Spanish folklore told of a group of seven priests who fled Spain after the invasion by the Moors in the early sixth century. The priests were said to have sailed west, where they established wealthy churches in cities with streets paved of gold. When the Spanish arrived in the New World, they found fabulous hoardes of gold, silver and jewels in both Central and South America. The Indians in these places told stories of northern cities with streets of gold, and the Spanish concluded they were the same Seven Cities from the old Spanish legends; they spent vast sums of money, and lost many lives, in quests for these riches.

Exploration of the Southwest by Spanish explorers began without auspicious results. The first explorers through the region found it of little economic interest and were unsuccessful in fulfilling their goals of adding wealth to the Spanish crown. After more than 700 years of conflict with the Moors, Spain emerged in the 15th century as the most powerful nation in Europe and felt it was their destiny to conquer the world in the name of the Spanish Crown and the Catholic Church.

The arrival of Christopher Columbus in the New World in 1492 started a chain of events that would forever change life on the American continents. Aided by far superior weaponry, horses for mobility, a thirst for conquest, and the belief that theirs was a mission for the greater glory of God, the Spaniards conquered the Americas in what was actually an extension of the Crusades. In 1493, Pope Alexander VI presented Spain with a papal bull, granting it title to all lands discovered west of the Azores as long as the lands discovered were held in the name of the Catholic Church.

Christopher Columbus arrived in the West Indies and established the first European fort, called La Navidad, on December 26, 1492, after his flagship, the Santa Maria, ran aground on a coral reef off the coast of Haiti. Columbus left 39 of his men to construct the fort and resumed his explorations. As always with early Spanish explorers, he was in search of gold and other material wealth. On his second voyage in 1493, with a fleet of 17 ships and more than 1,200 men, he found the fort burned and all his men dead. Some, according to the Indians,

had been killed by hostile natives and others had died from disease. Columbus left Haiti and sailed east for seventy miles to the island of Hispaniola where he established the first European town, which he named La Isabella for the Spanish Queen who was his benefactor, and again set out with hopes of discovering gold. Columbus ruled his West Indies kingdom with a harsh hand, against both the natives and members of his own expedition.

The Taino Indians of Hispaniola revolted after one of their chiefs and two of his companions were seized by Spaniards in retaliation for the theft of clothing. One Indian's ear was cut off and the other two were sent in chains to La Isabella. The Taino, who had begun relations with the Spanish in a spirit of friendship, were soon decimated by the Spaniards' European diseases for which they had no immunities, a pattern that continued throughout Spanish exploration and conquest of the New World.

The mayor of La Isabella, Francisco Roldãn, led a revolt against Columbus in 1497, which led to the end of La Isabella in 1498. In 1500, Columbus was returned to Spain in chains to face charges of enslaving Indians against the orders of the King and Queen; the ruthless execution of Spaniards who disobeyed him; and refusing to give supplies to those who displeased him. Columbus was acquitted for his crimes, but was never restored to the leadership of the West Indies. Although he was allowed to lead another expedition, a succession of other Spanish explorers quickly conquered most of South and Central America. Unfortunately, a pattern of distrust between the Indians and

Left: Mission San Xavier del Bac, near Tucson, Arizona. The original mission was established by Father Eusébio Francisco Kino, a Jesuit missionary, in 1700, but was burned to the ground in the Pima Revolt of 1751. The existing church was completed by the Franciscans in 1797, thirty years after the Jesuits were expelled from the New World in 1767 by King Carlos III of Spain.
PHOTO BY JACK W. DYKINGA

Right: Montezuma Canyon, at Coronado National Memorial in the Huachuca Mountains of southern Arizona. The area is believed by many to be the first place Spanish conquistador Francisco Vásquez de Coronado and his expedition crossed into the American Southwest, in June of 1540.
PHOTO BY JEFF GNASS

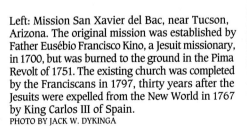

the Europeans began. A reputation for poorly managing the lands they conquered, and for gross mistreatment of their Indian subjects, remained with the Spanish throughout their involvement in the New World.

During the sixteenth century an estimated 200,000 Spaniards crossed the Atlantic to find fortune in the New World. Hernãn Cortes subdued the powerful Aztec Empire of Mexico in less than three years, and the Mayans, Toltecs and other Indian cultures in South and Central America followed in short succession. In 1532, Francisco Pizarro conquered the Incas of Peru, capturing 13,400 pounds of gold and 26,000 pounds of silver, along with countless other treasures in the ransom of the Inca chieftain Atahualpa (whom he ordered killed anyway), and twice these amounts when he conquered the Inca capital, Cuzco, in 1533.

The huge fortunes gained by conquistadors in South and Central America were the driving force behind Spanish expeditions in what later became the American Southwest. By 1519, a Spanish captain under orders of the governor of Jamaica had mapped the coast of Texas. In 1528, two expeditions under the command of Hernãn Cortes ventured across the Rio Grande into southern Texas for short excursions. In the same year, an expedition led by Pánfilo de Narváez set upon the shores of Florida at Tampa Bay. The ill-fated party left Spain in June of 1527 with 600 men and 80 horses. They encountered little difficulty in crossing the Atlantic Ocean, but reaching Santo Domingo nearly twenty-five percent of the men deserted in protest of the command by a difficult Narváez. Sixty more men and two ships were lost in a trip to Trinidad and Cuba for new recruits and additional supplies when they sailed into a hurricane. Narváez and his expedition were forced to spend the winter in Cuba for repairs to the remainder of his fleet and rest for his already weary men.

Narváez had previously been sent to Mexico by the governor of Cuba to relieve Cortes of his command when it became apparent he was planning to keep the riches of the Aztec empire for himself. Although Narváez was in command of a stronger force, he was no match for the cunning of Cortes and remained a prisoner of Cortes for three years. Embittered by losing such a spectacular prize, Narváez became determined to find the riches he so desperately desired, a trait that was to prove his undoing and had disastrous consequences for his entire expedition as well.

As was the custom of the Spanish Crown during this period, a Treasurer was appointed to insure that the King collected his royal fifth, the customary 20 percent of captured wealth levied as a tax to the Spanish King. The treasurer, Alvar Nuñez Cabeza de Vaca, was to undergo one of the most extraordinary adventures of all time during the next eight years.

Events unfolded disastrously for the Narváez Expedition from the moment they set out from Cuba at the end of February. They were down to five ships, 400 men and 40 horses. Upon landing in Florida Narváez immediately set out to find the fabled Seven Cities that played a fascinating dual role in both the legends of the Spanish (and Moors) and the various native tribes that earlier Spanish expeditions had encountered. So great were these legends, and so rich the treasures that had already been found in Central and South America, that no one even doubted their existence. Narváez believed even greater treasures than those seized from Montezuma and the Aztecs by Cortes must surely await him at every turn. This obsession caused him to pursue a series of events that were to prove disastrous.

Chasing after unfounded rumors of gold throughout the swamp lands of Florida, with

Above: The church at Mission San Jose at San Antonio Missions National Historical Park was built between 1768 and 1782 and is one of the finest examples of Spanish mission architecture found in the United States.
PHOTO BY GEORGE H. H. HUEY

Left: Interior of the Chapel of San Miguel in Santa Fe, New Mexico. San Miguel is one of the oldest churches in North America.
PHOTO BY TOM TILL

no results, Narváez then decided to continue inland from the coast and to send his ships ahead to find a safe harbor. Cabeza de Vaca vigorously opposed this as an unsound plan, but was eventually forced to accompany the expedition in order to fulfill his duties as Treasurer and to protect his honor. The ships sailed north, never finding the expedition again, just as Cabeza de Vaca had predicted.

During a year of searching the coast and swamps of Florida's Tampa Bay, the only trace of the expedition was found in a gruesome manner. Four men went ashore to question some seemingly friendly Indians, who seized them and forced three of the men to run the gauntlet while the Indians shot arrows at them. The fourth, a young boy named Juan Ortiz, was reprieved, because of his age, after being slowly roasted over a fire. He turned native and later escaped slavery to live with

that dwindled their numbers. As they encountered peaceful tribes, the Spaniards quickly abused their status as guests and hostilities would break out. Finally, after disease decimated a third of the expeditions still remaining numbers, it was then agreed that the only way to safety was to leave the swamp lands and take to the sea in boats. Somehow, they were able to build five boats that could hold up to fifty men each. The crafts were loaded with men and the remaining supplies, and made their way with continual hardship to the Gulf of Mexico. Upon crossing the mouth of the Mississippi River, the expedition continued to fall apart. One boat was swept to sea and was never heard from again. Narváez, whose boat held the most provisions and had the strongest

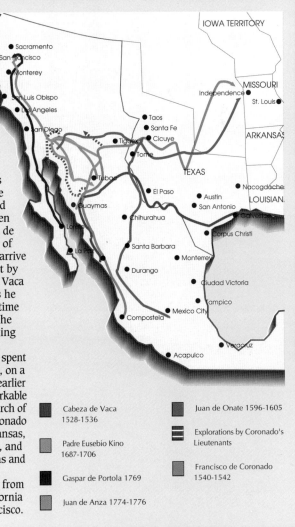

Above: Established in 1731, Mission Concepción in San Antonio Missions National Historical Park is the oldest unrestored stone Catholic church in the United States.
PHOTO BY TOM TILL

rowers was asked by Cabeza de Vaca to save the crew of his boat and another that was still within sight, to which Narváez replied it was

Above: Detail of a facade at Lady of Guadalupe Church at Mission San Juan, San Antonio Missions National Historical Park, San Antonio, Texas.
PHOTO BY GEORGE H. H. HUEY

a neighboring tribe. He was discovered eleven years later by Hernán de Soto on his expedition in Florida to find the Seven Cities. He was to prove an able interpreter and recounted the reasons for the Indians unfriendly behavior. In his quest, Narváez had captured the Indian's chief and cut off his nose, and then forced him to watch his mother being torn apart by the savage dogs the Spaniards traveled with. This had sealed his shipmate's fate when they were lured ashore a year later.

After searching for a year, all but one of the ships, which had been shipwrecked, found their way to safety. Narváez, Cabeza de Vaca and the rest of the shore party were not so fortunate. Time and again they encountered hostile tribes

SPANISH EXPLORATION OF THE WEST

Most Spanish explorations were made in the pursuit of material wealth, although some were made by dedicated missionaries like Father Kino who traveled throughout the Southwest, lived an impoverished life, and worked to better the lives of all he encountered.

Cabeza de Vaca, lost in the wilderness for eight years after being stranded with the Narváez Expedition in Florida, overcame tremendous obstacles to make his way through the wilderness of the southern and southwestern United States and return to his countrymen in Mexico. Along the way, Cabeza de Vaca learned that the best chance of survival in Indian country was to arrive with the sign of the cross, and not by brandishing a musket. Cabeza de Vaca became so beloved by the Indians he met in the southwest that by the time he rejoined his people in Mexico, he had a group of 600 Indians traveling with him as an admiring escort.

Francisco Vásquez de Coronado spent two years exploring the Southwest, on a route partially traveled two years earlier by Fray Marcos de Niza and a remarkable negro slave named Estebán, in search of the fabled Seven Cities of Gold. Coronado chased his dream as far east as Kansas, returned to Mexico empty-handed, and was tried for mistreating the Indians and mismanaging the expedition.

Juan Bautista de Anza traveled from Tubac, Arizona, overland to California and founded the city of San Francisco.

Cabeza de Vaca 1528-1536

Padre Eusebio Kino 1687-1706

Gaspar de Portola 1769

Juan de Anza 1774-1776

Juan de Onate 1596-1605

Explorations by Coronado's Lieutenants

Francisco de Coronado 1540-1542

now time for each man to look out for himself. Narváez crossed the mouth of the mighty river only to be swept away several days later and was never seen again. Thirty men remained in Cabeza de Vaca's party. When they attempted to regain the sea after putting ashore for provisions from a friendly Indian tribe, their boat was swamped causing the loss of three more men, their clothes, and all of their remaining provisions. Taking refuge with the Indians, they learned that two of the other captains, Andrés Dorantes and Alonso de Castillo, had survived and were in a neighboring Indian village. The two groups reunited, with combined forces then numbering around eighty men.

Unfortunately, winter set in and the meager food supplies of the Indians began to dwindle. So desperate were the Spaniards that some resorted to cannibalism. Many others died instead from starvation and disease. By spring, only fifteen members of the original group remained alive. Thirteen of these men, excluding Cabeza de Vaca who had temporarily fallen ill, set out across land to try and reach Spanish settlements in Mexico.

Recovering, Cabeza de Vaca traveled through the wilderness, trading with natives he encountered along the way for food and shelter. Four years later he came upon Castillo and Dorantes who had survived, along with a Negro slave called Estebán, but were being held as slaves in a neighboring Indian village. The four men, all that remained of the original expedition,

Above: Mission Espada, San Antonio Missions National Historical Park, is one of five Spanish missions found in San Antonio, the most of any city in the United States. Mission Espada was moved from an earlier site in east Texas, where it had been established in 1690. The mission's original adobe structure no longer remains. The mission seen here was begun in 1756 but was never completed. PHOTO BY DICK DIETRICH

escaped together and traveled through the barren lands. Once, while being held captive by a group of Indians, Cabeza de Vaca had been ordered to heal members of the Indian tribe.

Miraculously, he had accomplished this by making a sign of the cross, as was the Catholic custom. News of this feat spread across the land and wherever the four men went they were welcomed and asked to heal the sick. Time and time again, much to the amazement of the Spaniards, the Indians would recover.

By the time they reached the shores of the Rio Grande in South Texas, their trek had taken on all the aspects of a triumphal march. Finally, eight years after setting foot on the Florida shore, the four men, in the company of 600 Indian followers, came upon a Spanish slaver, Diego de Alcaráz, on a slaving expedition in northern Mexico. Alcaráz, although amazed by the sight of Cabeza de Vaca's appearance and vast entourage, attempted to enslave Indians traveling with de Vaca. Outraged, Cabeza de Vaca won the Indian's freedom through the aid of Melchior Díaz, the commanding officer of the nearest Spanish outpost.

Cabeza de Vaca and his group were escorted to the Governor of New Spain, Nuño de Guzmán, and from there to the Viceroy in Mexico City. Cabeza de Vaca had seen first hand the pitiful plight of the Indians throughout the lands where he had traveled. He had witnessed none of the fabled wealth of the Seven Cities of gold, but learned that the way to gain the Indians' friendship was through the sign of the cross, not through warfare or other acts of belligerence.

In tales of the journey of Cabeza de Vaca and his companions, the story was told of Indians to the north who lived in cities as fine as those found in Mexico. Governor Guzmán had long believed wealth equal to that found by Cortes must surely await discovery in the northern lands, a theory supported by Tejo, an Indian who was in Guzmán's possession. Tejo told the Spanish tales of a land to the north, where he had traveled with his father as a child, with large towns and abundant supplies of gold and silver. Tejo had himself seen seven very large cities, their streets filled with silver and gold. The search for the Seven Cities resumed again, this time as a project of the Viceroy, with an expedition that was led by a Franciscan friar named Marcos de Niza. Cabeza de Vaca had elected not to command the expedition and instead returned to Spain.

The Viceroy instructed Friar Marcos to treat the Indians with kindness and to demand that Spaniards he met along the way comply with his wishes, and that all Indians who were at peace were not be disturbed or forced

Left: Mission San Francisco de Assisi in Rancho de Taos, New Mexico, was built around 1730 by the Franciscans to convert the Taos Indians. PHOTO BY TOM TILL

into labor. He also ordered Friar Marcos to report to the new Governor, Francisco Vasquez de Coronado, who had recently replaced the greedy and brutal Guzmán. Friar Marcos, in the company of Estebán, was to proceed beyond the northern frontier and pacify the natives, record their ways and their flora and fauna, and take possession of the lands in the name of God and the Spanish Crown.

In March of 1539 Friar Marcos departed for the northern lands. Estebán was sent ahead to scout for the Seven Cities. When he learned of important news, he was to send Indians with a white cross back to the main party and report his position. Each time a white cross arrived, Marcos de Niza was sure he was nearing his destination. As they arrived at places from which Estebán had dispatched his messages, they always found him gone farther north in an apparent hurry. Indians both Estebán and Friar Marcos met along the way were familiar with the Seven Cities, the first of which they called Cíbola. From the Sonora Valley, Friar Marcos headed for the present-day border of Mexico and Arizona, which he crossed with little difficulty, just days behind Estebán.

When the Indians traveling with Friar Marcos assured him they were within a few days of Cíbola, the expedition was met with the horrifying news that Estebán had been killed, along with most of his entourage, upon reaching the city. The Indians in Friar Marcos' company refused to travel on. Only after much cajoling did he convince a party to lead him to where he could at least view the city for himself. He was led to a hill across from the city, which he later declared greater than Mexico City itself, and, choosing discretion over valor, marked the place with a cross that dedicated the lands to St. Francis, in the name of the Viceroy and the King. He then fled south to tell of the city

Above: San Jose de Garcia Church at Las Trampas in the Sangre de Christo Mountains of New Mexico was built in the 1700's with walls four feet thick.
PHOTO BY TOM TILL

that, in his mind, now only needed to be conquered. The city he discovered, in west-central New Mexico, was the Zuñi pueblo, Hawikuh.

Upon Friar Marcos' return with news that the Seven Cities, now the Seven Cities of Cíbola, had been found, waves of excitement spread through the Spanish world. The Viceroy prepared to send his most trusted protege to command an expedition but, being a prudent man, first sent Captain Melchior Díaz to trace the route of Friar Marcos. Díaz returned, not able to reach the Seven Cities of Cíbola because of bad weather, and with the less than exciting news that, although the local Indians verified the cities' existence, and that there were large multi-storied buildings and an abundance of turquoise, none had ever

seen gold or silver in any quantity. Although the report's contents were secret and for the Viceroy's knowledge only, the news leaked and Friar Marcos was forced to assure members of the expedition of the riches that awaited.

April 22, 1540, Francisco Vasquez de Coronado led the Viceroy's expedition into the Southwestern region of the United States. Coronado, along with 336 Spaniards, around 1,000 Indian allies, 1,500 horses and mules and numerous cattle and sheep, was in the company of four friars, with Marcos de Niza at their head. The expedition is thought to have first entered the United States at a point near Coronado National Monument in southeastern Arizona.

Upon arriving at the Zuñi pueblo Hawikuh, Coronado and his men were led into an ambush but quickly overcame the resistance they encountered and captured the city. Upon inspection of their prize, they were gravely disappointed at the lack of material wealth they surveyed. Indeed, the buildings were of high quality, just as Friar Marcos had said, but no sign of gold or silver was found.

THE SEARCH FOR THE SEVEN CITIES OF GOLD

Legends of the fabled Seven Cities of Gold were first told in Spain of a group of seven priests who had escaped from Spain following the Moorish invasion in the seventh century. The priests were said to have traveled west to an island, far from the Spanish shores, where they built seven churches, each in its own city that was so rich the streets were paved with gold. Variations of this story were told placing the Carthaginians on the island in ancient times; Spanish ships coming close to but not landing on the island in 1414; and Prince Henry the Navigator's sailors landing on the island and discovering grains of pure gold on its beaches.

Spanish explorers and nobility alike were inclined to believe these tales, especially after landing in Central and South America where conquistadors captured fabulous fortunes from splendid cities ruled by the Aztecs, Incas and Mayans. Spanish and Portuguese Kings granted rights to capture and claim the Seven Cities to a number of explorers with great seriousness.

Cartographers of the day placed the Seven Cities at various points on maps, first on islands, which some labeled as floating in the sea, and later, after Spanish exploration of the Caribbean failed to turn up the Seven Cities, placed them on the mainland from Florida to points in the west.

Throughout the Spaniards' conquered lands they heard stories from natives of Seven Cities, reportedly rich in gold and with large houses. Some referred to these cities as the Seven Cities of Cíbola, giving them a name. There were many Indians who were certain of their location, which was always just a little further than the Spaniards' present camp. Others had either been to these great cities or had friends, or relatives, that had visited or conducted trade with the wealthy people of the Seven Cities. The Spaniards were an eager audience for these tales, sure that

Coronado upon his arrival in New Mexico.
MURAL BY GERALD CASSIDY COURTESY MUSEUM OF NEW MEXICO

the wealthy cities awaited within their reach, and many believed they were one in the same as the Seven Cities of their own legends.

Even after the eight year journey of Cabeza de Vaca, from Florida to the Southwest and south to Mexico, during which he encountered only Indians of extreme poverty and bare subsistence levels, Spanish Governor Nuño de Guzmán still spent his own fortunes chasing stories spun by an Indian in his possession, named Tejo, of Seven Cities where his father had traded ornaments for large quantities of gold and silver.

Francisco Vasquez de Coronado, after hearing tales by Fray Marcos de Niza, who had witnessed the great walls of the city of Cíbola but had not entered because the Indians were violent, led a massive expedition throughout the Southwest in search of the Seven Cities of Cíbola. Arriving at Fray Marcos' city, the Zuñi Pueblo Hawikuh, Coronado found few items to interest him. Ever sure of his quest, Coronado followed a dubious Indian the Spaniards called "The Turk" clear into Kansas before finally realizing he had been duped.

Coronado held council with the Indian's leaders and determined from them that several larger cities existed to the northwest, in the land of the Hopi, and that pueblos of substantial size also existed to the east. During the meeting two Indians arrived from a Towa village along the Pecos River to the east. Stories of large cities to the east raised Coronado's hopes that great wealth would surely be found.

He dispatched an expedition of men to the northwest to search for the Hopi villages and to verify the rumors of a great river that might prove navigable, so that the ships of Hernando de Alarcón, who had been dispatched by the Viceroy with additional supplies for Coronado's vast army of conquerors, could find passage that would allow them access to the region. Another party was led east by the Indians from the Towa village so they could discover what lay in that direction.

Melchior Díaz was dispatched southwest with Friar Marcos, now suspected by many to have fabricated much of his earlier report on the region, to try and make contact with the supply ships. Díaz reached the lower Colorado River but arrived too late to meet the supply ships of Hernando de Alarcón, who had been able to navigate the Colorado River only as far north as Yuma.

On August 25, 1540, Coronado sent twenty-five men, under the command of Captain Garcia Lopez de Cardenas, north to the lands of the Colorado Plateau to investigate stories of the great river and the Indians who were thought to possess great wealth. Cardenas and his party arrived at the Grand Canyon, probably in an area on the South Rim, and found neither the

gold they were seeking nor the river itself. Disappointed, they neglected to even name this giant abyss and returned to Coronado.

Pedro de Tovar led a small force to the Hopi Mesas, which the Spanish called Tusayan, and

Above: Acoma Pueblo, or Sky City, one of the oldest continually inhabited villages in the New World. When the Spaniards arrived, in 1540, they were unable to scale the more than 400 foot high cliffs to the pueblo, although they killed around 100 Acoma men in their attempt. In 1598, the pueblo submitted to Spanish rule, but shortly thereafter killed Juan de Zaldivar, a nephew of Juan de Oñate, who was then Spanish governor of New Mexico, and twelve soldiers who accompanied him. Zaldivar's death was avenged by the killing of more than 100 Acoma men, and the kidnapping of 60 young Indian girls who were sold into slavery in Mexico.
PHOTO BY TOM TILL

camped during the night outside the first of seven villages they came upon. The Hopi were less than excited to see these strange foreigners

and attacked with bows and wooden clubs. No match for the Spaniards on their horses, they were quickly routed and decided upon a friendlier approach. After trading cotton cloth and turquoise items with the Spaniards, items that were of little interest to the explorers, they were left in peace until 1629 when Friar Porras, a Franciscan missionary, arrived with a military escort and began building churches, schools and convents at Oraibi, Shongopovi and Awatovi. An uneasy period of contact between the cultures lasted until the Hopi joined the other Pueblos in the 1680 Revolt that drove the Spanish from Indian lands. The Spanish never gained substantial footholds on the Hopi Mesas again.

Coronado's eastern expedition, led by Hernando de Alvarado, reached the Rio Grande in New Mexico and the Tiguex Pueblos, today called Tiwa. There was no sign of the gold and silver they sought, nor was there any at the other pueblos they visited on the journey that ventured as far east and north as Taos, New Mexico. Alvarado sent Coronado word that although no gold or silver had been found, the area at Tiwa was fertile and the Indians peaceful. Coronado's entire army marched east to spend the winter along the Rio Grande in Tiguex, an area that later developed into Albuquerque.

The expedition's stay at Tiguex during the winter taxed the patience of the Pueblos. The Spaniards were ill-equipped for the winter and soon appropriated one of the Tiwa pueblos for their own use. Without adequate clothing, they began to strip winter clothing from the Indians. After three months of tolerating the Spaniards' presence, which included suffering their arrogance and violation of the Indian women, the Tiwas revolted. A sustained period of warfare occurred that found the Spaniards, although they were eventually the victors, in a less than tenable position. After the Tiwas capitulated, the Spanish decided that an example needed to be set for all of the Pueblos to witness. Thirty Indians were burned at the stake, and pueblos that were not ruined during the fighting were looted and burned to the ground. By Spring, the Tiwas were forced to abandon their villages and retreat to the nearby mountains. When the Spaniards were forced to spend another winter in Tiguex, it was without the benefit of the Tiwa storehouses. When the members of the expedition returned to Mexico, Coronado and his second-in-command were to face trial for abusing the Indians. The Spaniards did not return to the Tiwa province for another

CORONADO AND THE TURK

By the time Coronado's first expedition to the Pueblos of New Mexico, led by Hernando de Alvarado, arrived at the Pecos Pueblo, hope was running out that the Seven Cities of Cíbola were filled with gold and silver. Their Indian guide, Chief Bigotes, had grown tired of the excursion and asked to be relieved of his duties. He gave the Spaniards two of his personal slaves; Sopete, from a land called Quivira, and another Indian from a region called Harahey, who looked like a Turk, which the Spanish promptly named him.

While exploring the Great Plains, The Turk told tales of the riches of Quivira. The Turk claimed to have a bracelet made of solid gold from Quivira, which he said had been taken from him by his master, Chief Bigotes. He asked the Spaniards to make the chief return the bracelet, so they would know he was not lying.

Exploration of the plains was abruptly ended and the expedition returned to Pecos to question Bigotes, who denied ever seeing the bracelet. The Spaniards resorted to bullying tactics to force the chief to give them the bracelet, and when he still professed no knowledge of it, locked him and another chief in chains. The Indians, outraged at

such behavior toward their leaders, grew hostile. Alvarado took both chiefs and The Turk, all in chains, to meet with Coronado at Tiguex.

Coronado was fascinated by The Turk's stories of Quivira, which included those of giant fish, a canoe rowed by forty men with a golden eagle on its prow, and ample quantities of gold and silver. The Turk now asked Coronado to make Bigotes return the bracelet so he would see that he was telling the truth. The two chiefs were taken to a field where savage dogs were turned on them. Still, they professed no knowledge of the bracelet.

In Spring, Coronado's party, led by The Turk, set out for Quivira. Along the way the other slave, Sopete, began to denounce The Turk as a liar and claimed he was purposely leading the expedition into oblivion. After weeks of searching, the Spaniards, now in Kansas, grew increasingly suspicious. The Turk, under intense questioning, broke down and confessed that he had lied.

Coronado did reach Quivira, but found none of the riches he desired. There, The Turk confessed that he had wished to lead the expedition into the wilderness so that they would die. For his duplicity, Coronado had The Turk strangled.

forty years. The Tiwa had no further contact with Spaniards until two Franciscans decided to remain in the region to preach the gospel to Indians after being warned against remaining by their military companions. The missionaries were indeed killed by the Indians. The Tiguex Pueblos were largely abandoned after the 1680 Revolt and were not resettled until the early 1700's. The absence of the Tiwas, many of whom moved to Arizona to live among the Hopis, allowed the Spanish to begin settling the Rio Grande Valley and to establish the town of Albuquerque, New Mexico.

The unsettling winter with the Tiwa could have ended Coronado's quest for the Seven Cities except for one further remarkable turn of events. During the winter an Indian the Spaniards called The Turk, for his resemblance to Turkish people, told tales of the riches of the kingdom of Quivera, that was supposedly filled with gold and silver. (See sidebar "Coronado and the Turk.") It seems hard to imagine that the Spanish could be led on yet another wild goose chase, except that their overwhelming desire for the riches they still believed lay just around the next bend, must have clouded their somewhat questionable judgement.

Coronado personally led the expedition to Quivera, which took him through Oklahoma and into Kansas, where he finally realized he had been duped. The expedition returned to spend a second miserable winter in Tiguex. In the Spring of 1542, Coronado and his forces began the long trek back to Mexico City. Upon his return he was charged with gross cruelty to the Indians and criminal mismanagement of the expedition. Found guilty, he was relieved as governor of Nueva Galica. A review board later reversed the charges, but Coronado was never to recover from his disappointments, dying a broken man at the age of forty-four. Coronado's expeditions marked an end to the search for the Seven Cities in the Southwest, as the Spanish Crown ordered that no further expeditions made in this nonproductive field.

Below: The ruins of three Spanish churches built between the late 1600's and 1820 are preserved in Tumacacori National Historical Park in Arizona. The first mission was established here in 1687 by a Jesuit, Father Eusébio Francisco Kino.
PHOTO BY JACK W. DYKINGA`

SPANISH MISSIONARIES AND SETTLERS...

After the futile attempts to locate the Seven Cities and other sources of wealth failed, Spanish exploration passed from the hands of the conquistadors to the Spanish Franciscan missionaries and the new breeds of treasure hunters, Spanish miners and settlers. Forty years after Coronado's retreat, Friar Agustin Rodriguez led the first expedition into New Mexico's Rio Grande Valley. Father Agustin and two other Franciscans were joined by a group of nine soldiers, all of whom happened to be miners. Upon reaching the Pueblos, the friars were content to save native souls while the soldiers explored surrounding areas, west to Zuñi and east to the plains, to locate potential mining sites. When the soldiers were ready to return to Mexico to report their favorable findings, Father Agustin and another friar elected to stay behind to continue converting the Indians, much to the dismay of the soldiers who had been retained to protect them.

A rescue mission was launched by Antonio de Espejo and a Franciscan friar, but it was too late and they discovered the two Franciscans had been killed by the Indians. Undismayed, Espejo visited many of the Rio Grande Pueblos and searched for mining sites, traveling as far west as the Verde Valley in Arizona.

In 1598 Spain finally decided to colonize New Mexico and selected Juan de Oñate as its first governor. Oñate's expedition explored as far west as the Gulf of California and as far east as Kansas. Juan de Oñates conquest was a peaceful one, except when he found his nephew, Juan de Zaldivar, and the twelve soldiers who had accompanied him, killed by Indians at Acoma. Juan de Oñate avenged their deaths by killing

Above: A traditional pueblo oven at Taos Pueblo, New Mexico. The Taos Indians have lived in Taos Pueblo for nearly 1,000 years. Taos is the largest existing multi-storied Pueblo structure in the United States. Taos Pueblo was first visited by the Spanish in 1540 when Hernando de Alvarado led Coronado's first eastern expedition.
PHOTO BY TOM TILL

more than 100 Acoma men, and kidnapping 60 young Indian girls who were then sold into slavery in Mexico. The trail Oñate forged in 1598, from Chihuahua, Mexico, to the Rio Grande Valley in New Mexico, became known as El Camino Real, and was the first commercial European trail in the United States.

Oñate's first settlement, at San Gabriel, ended in failure. In 1610, Santa Fe was established as the capital of New Mexico by Governor Pedro de Peralta. The fledgling province existed in a state of uneasy peace with its Pueblo Indian inhabitants until 1680.

The Indians, in a majority of the Pueblos, had been set upon by zealous Spanish missionaries forcing them to labor building churches, convents and schools. The Spanish Fathers had little tolerance for the Indians' most sacred traditions and destroyed many kivas and other items they felt were objects of idol worship. Occasionally, Indians would retaliate for the Spanish excesses, always to be met with military force and subdued. In 1680, for the first time in their history, the Indians of all the Pueblos, and some groups of Apaches, joined forces to face a common enemy, the Spaniards.

Plans for the Pueblo Revolt of 1680 were drafted by Po-pe, the leader of the Taos Pueblo. Messengers were sent throughout the land with cords tied with knots used to represent the number of days that remained until all the Pueblos would rise against their oppressors. The Indians quickly routed the Spaniards, but surprisingly killed only about 20 friars and around 400 others, allowing the great majority of Spaniards to retreat. The Indians were not after blood; they wanted only their lands back and freedom to practice their own religion and customs.

The Spaniards retreated to El Paso, Texas, where they remained for the next twelve years. With the exception of a few unsuccessful raids to recapture the territory, they left the Indians in peace. In 1692, the Spanish, under command of Governor Diego de Vargas, entered New Mexico and, in a bloodless campaign that promised amnesty and better treatment for the Indians, brought the territory back under Spanish control. The future was not without strife; the following year when Vargas returned, with around 1100 settlers and 18 Franciscan Friars to re-colonize the territory, he executed 70 Indians that had occupied the Governor's

Left: In 1540, Garcia Lopez de Cardenas, a captain in Coronado's army, led the first Europeans to the Grand Canyon. Finding neither the wealth they were searching for, nor access to the river below, they left unimpressed. It was more than 200 years before the next Spaniard, Father Francisco Tomas Garces, explored the area and descended into the canyon in 1776. Father Garces gave the Canyon its first European name, Puerto de Bucareli.
PHOTO BY JACK W. DYKINGA

palace in Santa Fe. The Pueblos believed that the Spaniards intended to punish them for the 1680 Revolt. Most retreated to the Mesas while others kept the Spaniards restricted to their fortifications. Finally, after a rebellion in 1696 that was unsuccessful, the two cultures found ways to co-exist, brought about mainly by changes in Spanish policy that forbade any kind of tribute exacted from the Indians. The Franciscans decided to be satisfied with an outward conversion to Christianity by the Indians, while allowing them to keep their kivas and traditional customs.

In 1681, after their retreat from the Pueblo Revolt of 1680, the Spanish built a mission at Ysleta del Sur, which is the oldest European settlement in Texas. In 1690, they entered east Texas and established a series of missions that were later moved to San Antonio. In 1718, the mission San Antonio de Valero, later to gain fame as the Alamo, was established, with four more missions rising in the San Antonio area over the following thirteen years.

In 1691, Father Eusébio Francisco Kino, a Jesuit missionary, began his travels throughout the Southwest. Kino established a series of missions in southern Arizona, including Guevavi (of which there are no remains), San Jose de Tumacacori and Mission San Xavier del Bac,

along with numerous settlements. Father Kino was beloved by all and was instrumental in introducing cattle ranching to his parishioners.

During the Spanish years of colonization, the most pressing problems they encountered were from the French, who claimed the Rio Grande as the western boundary of their Louisiana Territory, and Apache and Comanche Indians who continually raided their missions and settlements. By the middle of the 18th century the Spanish had settled their problems with the French and raiding Apaches, but faced grave problems from the Commanches, who had begun moving into the region when their mobility increased because of the introduction of Spanish horses, which they were known to steal. The Commanches destroyed the mission of San Saba de la Santa Cruz in 1759, killing the Spanish priests and mission Indians. The Comanche problem grew so intense that even the Apache sided with the Spanish to fight Comanches. In the ensuing battle, the Spanish and Apache were defeated, with the Spaniards withdrawing to central Texas to escape the continual Comanche attacks.

Indian raiding proved a continual problem throughout the Spanish occupation of the Southwest. Apache, Navajo, Comanche and Ute proved formidable adversaries against

the Franciscans, Jesuits and Spanish settlers. The continual raiding and Indian uprisings, including the Pima Rebellion in Arizona in 1751, and the Yuma Massacre by the Yuma Indians in 1781, strained Spanish resources.

In 1776, the Spanish were in desperate need of a northern route, away from hostile Indians, to their missions in California. Fathers Francisco Atanasio Domingues and Silvestre Velez de Escalante journeyed north from Santa Fe to the Dolores River in southern Colorado, which they followed to the Gunnison River and on to the White River, where they headed west to Utah in an unsuccessful search for a northern route to the California missions. The Spanish Fathers, Domingues and Escalante, were the first white men to enter Colorado and Utah.

The Spaniards never found the fabled riches they desired and were continually taxed with Indian problems; one must wonder if there were any tears shed in Spain in 1821 when Mexico won her independence and relieved the Spaniards of their lands in the Southwest.

Below: Ruins of the church at Quarai in Salinas Pueblo Missions National Monument, New Mexico. The national monument contains ruins of three missions built in the early 17th century, Abó in 1622, Quarai in 1626 and Gran Quivira in 1629.
PHOTO BY JACK W. DYKINGA

THE ANGLO ARRIVAL

The first Anglo-Americans in the Southwest were explorers, trappers and fur traders. These intrepid adventurers paved the way for a succession of merchants, miners and settlers, all of whom were threatened by hostile Indian tribes and expulsion by Spaniards. In 1821, Mexico won independence from Spain, and for the next twenty-five years the Southwest was ruled from afar by the Mexicans.

The Mexican government was not as threatened by the American traders, settlers and trappers as the Spaniards had been, and the Southwest was governed largely from Santa Fe, New Mexico. The Spaniards may have been wise in their attempts to limit Anglo intrusions, for soon Anglo settlers grew weary of Mexican rule. Texas independence from Mexico was won in 1836, beginning the end of Mexican rule in the Southwest.

Following the Mexican War of 1846, a chain of military forts was established that provided a modicum of security for settlers and ranchers. Skirmishes with the Indians were still a constant threat to the early pioneers, and it was not until completion of the Santa Fe Railroad that travel between Southwestern destinations and the rest of the country was free from Indian harassment.

The earliest Anglo-Americans to visit the Southwest were explorers, trappers and traders. Their expeditions paved the way for the frontiersmen and settlers that followed. The Spanish successfully prevented American and French intrusions into the Southwest until the early 1800's. It was illegal for subjects of the Spanish Crown in the Southwest to enter into trade with foreigners, and often traders and explorers who entered Spanish territory were arrested and summarily deported.

In July of 1805, Lieutenant Zebulon Pike led an expedition from St. Louis, across the plains of Kansas and the southern boundary of what was then the United States, and arrived in Pueblo, Colorado, in late November of 1806. Pike was accompanied by John H. Robinson, a civilian doctor, and twenty-one soldiers. Entering the eastern foothills of the Rockies, Lt. Pike, Robinson and two soldiers attempted to climb a mountain they encountered, which today bears the name Pikes Peak in honor of the young lieutenant, even though he was never able to reach its summit.

For reasons that are still unknown, Lt. Pike's expedition failed to pack adequate uniforms and equipment for winter survival. As winter in the Rockies set in, the intrepid group found themselves not only poorly equipped, but also very lost. The only map of the territories they were to explore had been drawn by a German, Alexander von Humboldt, who had never been to the region. Humboldt had drawn the map based on archives of frontier documents in studied in Mexico City. It was of little value to Pike and his men. In search of Santa Fe, the capital of New Spain, they rode through the southern areas of Colorado until their horses began to die. Pike had a shelter built for two men who were to stay with the remaining horses, while the balance of the expedition set out on foot in what they thought was the direction of Santa Fe. They continued to leave men, whose feet had become frozen, in crude shelters, promising to return for them, while they continued their search.

Reaching the Rio Grande, in the Spanish territory that is now New Mexico, they built a stockade and sent men back along their trail to pick up those they had left behind. John Robinson, who had proved the heartiest member of the expedition, set out to Santa Fe for help. Robinson would surely have perished if not for the help of a band of Ute Indians who led him to Taos, for he was travelling well away from the route to Santa Fe, once again relying on Humboldt's map.

From Taos, Robinson was taken to Santa Fe where authorities quickly sent troops to the site of Lt. Pike's stockade. The New Mexican government was not sure what to do with Pike and his men, who were uniformed soldiers of a country that was at peace with Spain, but who were unwelcome in the territory. The Spanish authorities were convinced they were spies, and many historians believe this may indeed have been the case. Pike and his group were sent south to Chihuahua, Mexico, where they were questioned further. Finally, Zebulon Pike's notes of the journey were confiscated and the expedition was led across the deserts of Chihuahua to the southeastern Texas border

Preceding Pages: Paria Canyon, Vermilion Cliffs Wilderness. Sunrise captures the textures and colors of eroded sandstone and petrified sand-dune formations.
PHOTO BY JACK W. DYKINGA

Left: Moran Point, Grand Canyon National Park. Moran Point was named for English artist Thomas Moran, an English artist who sketched the area while serving on Major John Wesley Powell's second expedition down the Colorado River.
PHOTO BY JACK W. DYKINGA

Right: The Trade Room at Bent's Old Fort National Historic Site, Colorado. From 1833 until 1845 the fort was an important meeting place for Indians, Americans and Mexicans. In 1845, Bent's Fort was commandeered by the Army of the West, under the command of General Stephen Kearny, for use by the United States in the Mexican War of 1846. In 1849, fire destroyed much of the fort, which was restored by the National Park Service during the 1970's.
PHOTO BY GEORGE H. H. HUEY

where they were released. Miraculously, all but one member of the expedition survived. In 1810, Zebulon Pike's published accounts of his journey through the Southwest, written entirely from memory since his journal had been confiscated by the Mexican authorities, became incredibly popular and soon cries of "Pike's Peak or Bust" were heard throughout the East as the insatiable desire of the Anglo-Americans for unsettled frontiers continued to fuel expeditions into the region.

Zebulon Pike's written adventures inspired several expeditions, many as unsuccessful as his own. Traders in the frontier towns of the United States were experiencing problems in moving trade merchandise from their shelves; many thought the Southwest would prove to be an untapped source of new profits. Traders Robert McKnight and James Baird purchased $10,000 worth of the dry goods that Pike had written of as being potentially profitable, only to have them confiscated by Spanish authorities when they arrived in New Mexico. Their goods were auctioned off to pay for the imprisonment costs of the entire expedition.

In September of 1821, William Becknell of Missouri led a small trading expedition to Santa Fe, where he was met in a favorable light by New Mexico authorities. His trade goods were promptly sold and he returned to Missouri, laden with silver coins, to acquire additional items to trade. Becknell, through trial and error on successive trips, established the Santa Fe Trail. Soon, Anglo traders, trappers and settlers were traveling the Santa Fe Trail into the Southwest.

The arrival of Zebulon Pike also influenced the fate of the state of Texas. Spanish officials offered huge land grants to *empresarios* who would settle in the remote regions of Texas, to counter continuing pressure from American settlers and hostile Indians. Even this grandiose scheme backfired when the Southwest came under Mexican rule. In 1821, Mexican officials decided to honor the *empresario* status Spain had granted to Moses Austin. Although he died after receiving Spanish government permission to develop a huge tract of land, but before he had a chance to develop it, he was also the father of Stephen Fuller Austin who inherited his father's rights and was eventually responsible for fostering a population of more than 5600 Texans by 1831. Austin was later a major catalyst in Texas' bid for independence.

In Arizona, early fur traders, mineral prospectors and trappers traveled the mountain and plateau regions of the state searching for precious metals and beaver pelts, which were in great demand for use in men's hats. In 1826, James Ohio Pattie visited the regions of the Colorado Plateau, including the Grand Canyon area, and wrote of his adventures in the popular book,

"Personal Narrative." In 1828, George C. Yount led trapping expeditions through the mountain regions of Arizona and was reported to have reached the floor of the western Grand Canyon by descending the Spencer River.

Above: Sunrise on Bent's Fort, Bent's Old Fort National Historic Site, Colorado. Charles and William Bent, with partner Ceran St. Vrain, built the fort as headquarters for their trading company in 1833. The Bent, St. Vrain and Company was actively engaged in trade throughout the West and Southwest.
PHOTO BY GEORGE H. H. HUEY

Following Mexican independence from Spain in 1821, Anglo-Americans began to appear in ever increasing numbers in New Mexico. By 1826, legendary mountain man and Indian fighter Christopher "Kit" Carson had arrived in Taos, spending the winter with a mountain man known as Kincade, who taught the young Carson the basics of survival on the frontier. For the following two years, he signed on as a cook with the famous mountain man, Ewing Young, who was a teamster for the Santa Rita copper mine and a fur trapper. In August of 1829, Carson was finally signed on by Young as a trapper on an expedition that traveled through the Southwest to California.

Mountain man Jedediah Smith explored the regions of Utah long before any other non-Indian. Smith blazed the trail linking California with the rest of the country and became the first white man to cross the Sierra Nevada Mountains. Returning from an expedition to California in 1826, Smith and two companions, Silas Gobel and Robert Evans, entered Utah from Nevada, and traveled to the Great Salt

Left: The Rug Trader's Room at Hubbell Trading Post National Historic Site, Arizona. John Lorenzo Hubbell established the trading post at Ganado in 1878, after spending two years at a post he had established at Ganado Lake. Hubbell's customers were mainly Navajo Indians who were returning to the area after four years at the Bosque Redondo Reservation in New Mexico.
PHOTO BY GEORGE H. H. HUEY

Lake, nearly perishing in the harsh wilderness from lack of water. Smith was later killed by Comanches on the Santa Fe Trail. In 1836, Anglo trapper Denis Julien left his mark in what later became Utah's Canyonlands National Park. Julien carved his name and initials, along with the date, in several rocks from Desolation Canyon to Glen Canyon.

Accounts by these early mountain men and trappers led the way for the arrival of the Anglo merchants. Bringing wagon loads of trade goods, cloth, cooking utensils, dry foods, tools, shoes, nails, knives, guns and alcohol, these early merchants established a base of operations for all who followed. No longer were pioneers uncertain about finding much needed supplies along Southwestern routes.

In 1821, as the Mexicans were celebrating their independence, Missouri trader William Becknell had forged the route that later became the Santa Fe Trail. In 1831, brothers William and Charles Bent formed a trading company with Frenchman Ceran Saint Vrain, and built a fortress in the Arkansas River Valley of Colorado, which served as company headquarters. Bent, St. Vrain and Company engaged in trade throughout the Southwest and the West. William Bent managed the fort, Ceran Saint Vrain oversaw operations in Santa Fe, and Charles Bent spent much time traveling between the fort and company stores in Taos and Santa Fe. The company sold goods they imported from St. Louis, Navajo blankets, Mexican horses and numerous other items. The company's main warehouse operations were at Bent's Fort, now known as Bent's Old Fort National Historic Site, which also included a dining room, billiard room, guest accommo-dations, a blacksmith shop and a carpentry shop. This was a neutral site where Indians, Mexicans and Americans were all welcome. It became a major meeting center for all, and enjoyed a peaceful existence until it was commandeered by General Stephen Kearny's Army of the West for use in the Mexican War of 1846. Following the Mexican War, Kearny appointed Charles Bent as the first United States governor of New Mexico. Bent was killed and scalped within months by his constituents in the 1847 Taos Rebellion.

Below: The home of John Lorenzo Hubbell, built in 1901 at Hubbell Trading Post National Historic Site, Ganado, Arizona. Hubbell, with the help of partner C. N. Cotton, established 24 trading posts in the Southwest.
PHOTO BY GEORGE H. H. HUEY

THE TEXAS REVOLUTION...

Throughout the early 1800's, Texans rebelled against Hispanic rule. Spain had ceded the lands it occupied in the Louisiana Territory after the Louisiana Purchase of 1803, but was soon in a dispute with the U.S. over the boundary of New Spain. The American claims included Louisiana and all lands north and east of the Rio Grande after France had revived its claim of ownership of Texas, and sold the entire territory, including Texas, to the Americans.

President Thomas Jefferson purchased the Louisiana Territory from France, giving Americans a claim to Texas.

President Thomas Jefferson notified Spain that their people were expected to leave the territory, including Texas. Spain refused to withdraw from Texas and rushed troops to the border. The Americans, including the President, were eager to claim Texas. An uneasy peace between the two nations lasted until the region passed to Mexican control in 1821.

In 1812, Mexican revolutionaries joined with West Point graduate Lt. Augustus Magee, who had commanded the neutral zone between the countries before resigning his U.S. Army commission to declare himself a colonel in his own "Republican Army of the North."

The upstart army won control of Nacogdoches and La Bahia. When Magee died during a siege at La Bahia, and Samuel Kemper assumed the rank of colonel to replace him. Kemper led the army to victory in San Antonio, where he forced the Spanish to surrender at the Alamo.

The revolutionaries formed the "Republic of Texas" in April of 1813. They failed to gain recognition by foreign governments, including the U.S., and were soon vanquished when the Spanish Army regained control of San Antonio a few months later. Republican Army of the North members were tracked down by the Spaniards, who executed hundreds of them.

In 1826, Texans, led by *empresario* Haden Edwards, allied with the Cherokee Indians and formed the "Republic of Fredonia." Under Edwards' plan, Texas would be divided into two regions, one for Americans and one for Indians. The Mexican Army, with the aid of Anglo settlers who were against Edwards' plan, including the Texas militia and Stephen Austin, quickly ended the revolt. Austin, another *empresario*, had inherited his claim to Texas lands from his father, Moses Austin, who died before settling his land grant.

Under Mexican rule, the almost unlimited immigration of Anglos into Texas was allowed, and Anglo population swelled until immigration was outlawed in 1830. It was not most Texans'

Haden Edwards led the Fredonia Rebellion of 1826, which failed.

desire to seek independence, although they wanted the rights they had formerly enjoyed under the constitution of the United States.

Remarkably, it was General Antonio López de Santa Anna Pérez de Lebrón who led the revolt that ultimately led to sovereignty for Texas. Santa Anna led a rebellion in Mexico, calling for benefits and justice for all citizens of Mexico and a constitution similar to that of the United States. Texans were in favor of Santa Anna's revolt, as was the Mexican Army. Santa Anna was a hero in Mexico, the United States, Europe and even in Texas.

Texans were greatly mistaken in believing Santa Anna's reforms applied to them. They pressed for statehood during a convention in October of 1832. Stephen Austin was elected to lead the convention, which drafted resolutions asking the Mexican government to separate Texas into a state independent of Coahuila; to repeal Anglo immigration laws; for lands for schools; and for exemption from customs duties for a period of three years. They also declared their loyalty to Mexico. The Texans were convinced they had found an ally in General Santa Anna.

The Mexicans viewed the document as a plot against Mexican rule. Authorities in Coahuila did not send the resolution to Mexico City, informing the Texans

Stephen Fuller Austin, as an *empresario*, was responsible for settling thousands of people into Texas.

that even their meetings were against the law. News of the convention reached General Santa Anna, who denounced the Texans as foreigners seeking independence. A second convention in April of 1833 framed a constitution to be sent to the Mexican congress, a procedure followed in the United States by each new state that entered the Union. Its delivery was entrusted to Stephen Austin.

Mexican General Santa Anna was first viewed as a hero by Texans. He was later found to be a brutal dictator.

Austin met President Gómez Farías in July in Mexico City. Austin was at first well received, although months passed without action on the Texans' proposals. He told Farías that if the government would not organize a Texas state, Texans would do so themselves. He then sent a letter to officials in San Antonio suggesting formation of a state independent of Coahuila, where the ranking political officer considered the proposal treason and sent it to President Farías in Mexico City.

Meanwhile, Austin met Santa Anna who agreed to all Texan terms except statehood.

THE BATTLE OF THE ALAMO

The Alamo, a Spanish mission founded in 1718, was abandoned by 1793. It was used by the Spanish during the Mexican War for Independence and occupied from 1821 until 1835 by the Mexican Army.

Lt. Colonel William Barret Travis.

During the Texas Rebellion General Cós, the brother-in-law of Santa Anna, was forced to surrender the Alamo and his 1100 man army to a force of 300 Texans. Cós and his men were paroled after promising not to bear arms against Texas.

Cós' surrender enraged Santa Anna, who arrived in San Antonio on February 23, 1836, with around 5,000 men and a goal of executing or exiling all Texans who had a part in the rebellion. The next morning cannon fire pounded the Alamo, the beginning of a siege that lasted twelve days.

150 Texans were then inside the Alamo, commanded by William Travis, a lawyer who had arrived in February with about 30 men, and legendary knife fighter Jim Bowie had arrived from Goliad with another 30 volunteers. David Crockett, famous fighter and former congressman from Tennessee, and 12 of his men arrived February 8. Their forces

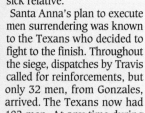

Jim Bowie, famous knife fighter.

joined about 100 men stationed at the Alamo, commanded by Lt. Colonel J.C. Neill, who left upon their arrival to tend a sick relative.

Santa Anna's plan to execute men surrendering was known to the Texans who decided to fight to the finish. Throughout the siege, dispatches by Travis called for reinforcements, but only 32 men, from Gonzales, arrived. The Texans now had 182 men. At any time during the siege, men could have slipped through enemy lines, but no one did.

David Crockett, the frontier legend, died at the Alamo.

On March 6, 1836, Santa Anna's army attacked the Alamo. Thousands of Mexican soldiers stormed the walls and the valiant defenders slain to a man. Travis was felled by a musket ball to the head. Jim Bowie was bayonetted in his sickbed, where he was dying of what was probably diphtheria. Davy Crockett's body was pierced by numerous bayonet wounds and found amidst a pile of slain Mexican soldiers.

The sizes of Mexican and Texan forces at the Alamo have long been debated by historians on both sides of the border. What is important is that a small band of Texans held vastly superior Mexican forces at bay, thereby gaining the time necessary to organize a defense of Texas.

Austin was satisfied by his meeting with Santa Anna and began the journey home. Upon his arrival in Coahuila, he was arrested under order of President Farías, who had finally received the letter Austin had tried to send to San Antonio, and was convinced the Texans were plotting a rebellion against the Mexican government.

Austin was returned to Mexico City and held in solitary confinement. Even as Austin was in prison, reforms Santa Anna had promised for Texas were granted and a new flood of immigration occurred. Texans were admitted to the congress, allowed for the first time to engage in retail trade, granted the right to their religion of choice, and authorized to have a superior court including trial by jury.

In April of 1834, Santa Anna ousted President Farías, assumed control of Mexico, dissolved

Sam Houston arrived in Texas in 1832 as an emissary of President Andrew Jackson. He remained and became a Texas citizen, troop commander, and was elected President of the Republic of Texas on two occasions.

the Republican Congress and replaced it with his own. He abolished local legislatures and voided the Constitution of 1824. Rebellions in the Mexican states of Coahuila and Zacatecas against the new policy were quickly subdued by Santa Anna's army.

Santa Anna's brother-in-law, General Martín Perfecto de Cós, was dispatched to Coahuila to end the uprising there. While in Coahuila, he sent a dispatch to the garrison at Anáhuac stating that the Mexican Army was on its way. The Texans were incensed, and sent William Barrett Travis, a lawyer originally from South Carolina, with a group of volunteers to capture Anáhuac. This was accomplished with a single shot from a cannon and without any bloodshed. Many Texan citizens were against this rebellious act, and expressed their loyalty to the government of Mexico. General Cós called for the arrest of all Texans, including Travis, who opposed the changes in the Mexican government. Even

The Mexican General Martín Perfecto de Cós, the brother-in-law of General Santa Anna, was routed from the Alamo by the Texans.

those who had desired peace were outraged. The call went out to form another convention, with a goal of securing peace if it could be obtained on constitutional terms, or declaring war if it could not.

Stephen Austin was released from prison in July of 1835, and given passage to New Orleans. He was now convinced Texas needed to secede from Mexico and issued a call for men and rifles to immigrate to Texas, sensing additional forces would soon be needed.

Upon Austin's return to Texas, he found matters had progressed far beyond his expectations. As a colonel of the militia, he chaired the San Felipe Municipal Committee of Safety. Within days, word arrived that General Cós and the Mexican Army had crossed the Rio Grande and were heading for San Antonio. Austin called the Texans to arms saying, "War is our only resource."

The war's first shots were exchanged after the Mexicans demanded the return of a cannon from settlers in Gonzales, Texas. The Texans flew a flag stating "Come and Take It," and then easily repelled the Mexicans' advance. The Mexican forces retreated to San Antonio, where they were forced to surrender after a five day siege. Nacogdoches, Anáhuac and Goliad were soon controlled by Texans. By the end of 1835, the Mexican Army had been driven from Texas.

Ben Milam, a 47 year old Welshman from Kentucky, led Texan forces to San Antonio to encounter General Cós' army. The third day of fighting, Milam died from a bullet to the forehead.

General Santa Anna was outraged and led more than 6,000 Mexican troops to Texas to quell the rebellion. A twelve day siege of the Alamo (see sidebar) defeated the Texans, at a tremendous cost to the Mexican Army, but gained valuable time necessary for an army, under Sam Houston's command, to prepare to defend the newly formed Republic.

Houston's army, of less than 1,000 men, charged Santa Anna's numerically superior forces near San Jacinto as they were taking their siesta. In less than 20 minutes, more than 600 Mexicans were killed at a cost of two Texans killed in battle and around 30 wounded. The Mexican Army surrendered. Santa Anna had escaped, fleeing as the attack first started, but was captured the next day and forced to negotiate peace with the Texans.

Left: The Alamo, originally Mission San Antonio de Valero, was a halfway point between northern Mexico and east Texas Spanish missions. During the Texas Rebellion, it was used as a fort by less than 200 Texans to fight thousands of Mexican soldiers under General Santa Anna's command.
PHOTO BY DICK DIETRICH

AMERICAN EXPLORATION OF THE GRAND CANYON...

American explorers were not the first Europeans to visit the Grand Canyon. Twenty-five Spaniards under the command of Captain Garcia Lopez de Cardenas were sent by Coronado to the region of the Colorado Plateau to verify stories of a great river and people who possessed great riches. Cardenas arrived at the rim of the canyon on August 25, 1540. Finding neither gold they were seeking, nor the river itself, they left disappointed, neglecting to even name the giant abyss.

The mouth of Black Canyon from the 1857 expedition of Lt. Joseph Christmas Ives.

It was more than 200 years before another Spaniard, Father Francisco Tomas Garces, explored the area. Garces descended into Havasu Canyon in 1776 and named the Grand Canyon Puerto de Bucareli in honor of the viceroy of New Spain.

Anglo-Americans were first to fully explore the area, to begin developing the resources of the Grand Canyon and to occupy the region. During the 1820's, American fur trappers, including James Ohio Pattie and George C. Yount, may have traveled through the Grand Canyon in search of beaver pelts, although there is no written record to substantiate their presence. In 1821, Mexico gained independence from Spain; thus control of New Spain, including the areas that later became the American Southwest, passed to Mexican hands for a period of twenty-seven years. With the signing of the treaty of Guadalupe Hidalgo in 1848, war with Mexico ended and the area became a territory of the United States. These two rapid changes in ownership did little to promote exploration of the Grand Canyon until President James Buchanan called for surveys of the area, for political reasons, in 1857.

President Buchanan ordered army troops to Utah as friction developed between the United

Geologist Dr. John Strong Newberry.
PHOTO COURTESY GRAND CANYON NATIONAL PARK I.D. NO.3332

States and the Mormons. Buchanan felt there was a strong possibility that the Mormons were in a state of rebellion and ordered the army to the area to ensure federal control. Searching for a way to supply troops in Utah from the south, army Lt. Joseph Christmas Ives, with the U.S. Army Corps of Topographical Engineers, was sent to find the northernmost point of steamship navigation on the lower Colorado River. The Ives Expedition arrived at the Grand Canyon in April of 1858.

After a cursory examination of the area, Ives continued his journey to Fort Defiance, in eastern Arizona, where he entered his report, concluding the Grand Canyon was valueless. In fact, Ives stated in his official report, "Ours has been the first and will doubtless be the last party of whites to visit this profitless locality."

Although Ives found very little economic or strategic value regarding the Grand Canyon, he was accompanied on the expedition by Dr. John Strong Newberry, a geologist who, in his written reports, became the first white man to ponder the Canyon and to question its geological formation. Newberry wrote of the physical features of the canyons, rocks, and fossils, and concluded that the river itself had eroded the Canyon. He was the first academic to describe the Canyon's wonders.

Maj. John Wesley Powell traversed the length of the Grand Canyon with the use of one arm; the other was lost during the battle of Shiloh.
PHOTO COURTESY GRAND CANYON NATIONAL PARK I.D. NO.5133

JOHN WESLEY POWELL'S GRAND CANYON EXPLORATIONS

On May 24, 1869, John Wesley Powell, a retired major in the Union Army who had lost his right arm during the Civil War at the Battle of Shiloh, set out to travel the length of the Colorado River through the Grand Canyon by boat. Major Powell, who had a background in the study of natural sciences and a particular interest in the field of geology, embarked on his famous journey from Green River, Wyoming. Green River was chosen because it was a stop on the Union Pacific Railroad, which had reached the area a few years before. With a railhead, the boats and all of the supplies needed for the expedition could easily be delivered to the starting point. Major Powell descended the Green River to the Colorado River with nine men in four pine rowboats. On the first leg of the journey one boat was destroyed and one member of the expedition declared that he had seen enough danger and quit.

The remaining members of Powell's expedition continued down the Colorado through Cataract Canyon, Glen Canyon and finally entered the Grand Canyon. While in the Grand Canyon, at what is now called Separation Rapid, three more men decided it was unsafe to continue and left the river to find an overland route to safety. This proved to be an unwise decision, for the three men were never seen again. At the end of the journey Major Powell sat in camp with his journal and wrote the following passage, "Now the danger is over; now the toil has ceased; now the gloom has disappeared; and what a vast expanse of constellations can be seen! The river rolls by us

Above: Two of the pine river boats of Powell's second expedition near the upper end of the Grand Canyon in 1872.
PHOTO COURTESY OF GRAND CANYON NATIONAL PARK. IDENTIFICATION NUMBER 5309

in silent majesty; the quiet of the camp is sweet; our joy is almost ecstasy. We sit till long after midnight, talking of the Grand Canyon, talking of home, but chiefly talking of the three men who left us. Are they wandering in those depths, unable to find a way out? Are they searching over the desert land above for water? Are they nearing the settlements?" Major Powell and his party, who had explored 1,048 miles in ninety-eight days, did not yet realize the three missing men would never be found. As time went by, the general consensus was that they were probably killed by a band of Paiute Indians living in the Grand Canyon area. No trace of their remains has ever been found.

Right: Map tracing Powell's first river expedition from Green River through Cataract Canyon, Glen Canyon and the Grand Canyon.

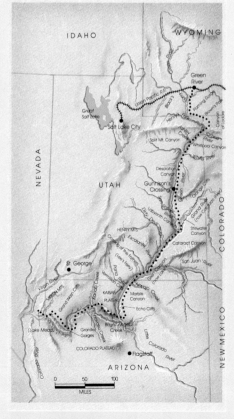

In the following ten years, small groups of prospectors roamed the Grand Canyon in search of mineral deposits. Like the conquistadors, it is possible their search for wealth kept them from noticing the Canyon's majestic beauty.

In 1869, John Wesley Powell, a former army major who had lost an arm in battle at Shiloh, undertook a bold and imaginative expedition to prove it was possible to navigate the Colorado River by boat along its entire canyon passages. Powell's well written accounts spurred the imagination of readers, then and now, and were a key factor in the continuing interest that developed in the Grand Canyon.

In 1870, Major Powell explored the northern areas of the Colorado Plateau while planning a second expedition down the Colorado River. In the Spring of 1871, Powell was sent by the federal government to map the Colorado Plateau and the Colorado River. More time was spent on this second expedition, and attention was focused on exploration of both sides of the river and surveying the canyon's area. The accounts of Major Powell's journeys were published in 1874, and soon gained wide readership in the U.S. and, after translation to foreign languages, across Europe. His were the first of many exciting river trips by adventurers from around the world that continue even today.

Clarence Edward Dutton, a protégé of Powell's, led the first major geological expedition of the Grand Canyon in 1880. Dutton conducted in-depth studies of the Canyon and wrote the first volume on the Canyon's geology. Dutton's book contained illustrations by Thomas Moran, an Englishman, who had also illustrated the area while serving as an artist on Powell's second expedition. Moran was not a member of the boat expedition down the Canyon and had to create his drawings from photographs taken by the expedition's photographer. Dutton, along with Major Powell, concluded that the river was older than the land forms it flowed through. They felt, erroneously, that prior to the formation of the Canyon today and, throughout the years, the river had cut its

way through the land, entrenching itself deeper and deeper as time flowed by.

English artist Thomas Moran sketching the Canyon. The official report of Major Powell's Expedition, entitled "The Exploration of the Colorado River of the West," included 29 of Moran's illustrations.
PHOTO COURTESY GRAND CANYON NATIONAL PARK I.D. NO.5309

Throughout the late 1880's, interest in the Grand Canyon continued to build. In 1882, and again in 1883 and 1886, Senator Benjamin Harrison of Indiana introduced bills to make the Grand Canyon a National Park. Though he was initially unsuccessful, Harrison was able to designate the area as the Grand Canyon Forest Reserve when he became President in 1893. Harrison's actions prevented the seizure of land by settlers.

In 1884, William Bass established a camp 27 miles west of the present Grand Canyon Village, near Havasupai Point. His competition for tourist lodgings was the Farlee Hotel, a one-room shanty that was opened the same year at the junction of Peach Springs Canyon and Diamond Creek. In 1886, John Hance, the first white settler on the South Rim, offered lodging at his ranch near Grandview Point. Hance was a colorful character and continued to offer his services as a guide and tour operator at the Canyon until his death in 1919. Known to tell tall tales, Hance once said, when asked about a missing tip of one of his fingers, that he had worn it off pointing it at the Grand Canyon.

J. Wilbur Thurber bought Hance's hotel in 1896, and the following year started construction on the Bright Angel Hotel in Grand Canyon Village. The Grand View Hotel opened its doors on the South Rim in 1897, becoming the first hotel to be located on the Canyon's rim. In 1904, El Tovar Hotel was built by the Fred Harvey Company, who bought the Bright Angel Hotel in 1906. President Theodore Roosevelt visited the Canyon in 1908 and was captivated by its beauty. Roosevelt established the Grand Canyon National Monument in 1908, which ensured a ban on prospecting and mining in the region.

President Theodore Roosevelt established the Grand Canyon National Monument in 1908.
COURTESY NATIONAL ARCHIVES

President Benjamin Harrison designated the Grand Canyon Forest Reserve in 1893.
COURTESY NATIONAL ARCHIVES

Right: The first rays of the sun's light at sunrise strike the Canyon's walls at Cape Royal on the North Rim of the Grand Canyon.
PHOTO BY CARR CLIFTON

THE UNITED STATES ARMY CONQUERS THE SOUTHWEST...

Following the Texas Rebellion, the Mexican government was not content to live up to its peace treaties. In 1842, the Mexican Army launched guerrilla raids against the cities of San Antonio, Refugio, Goliad and Victoria. Mexican troops, around 1400 strong, occupied San Antonio and proclaimed the reconquest of Texas until Captain Jack Hays and 600 Texas Rangers routed them from the city. Numerous skirmishes occurred on both sides of the border, and in neighboring New Mexico, which Texas and Mexico claimed as their own territory.

Captain Jack Hays of the Texas Rangers was responsible for introducing Samuel Colt's repeating pistol to the Southwest.

The Mexicans were less involved in the affairs of Arizona, New Mexico and the balance of the Southwest during their brief rule. They were content to let the governor of New Mexico make most of the major decisions affecting the territory. An expedition, authorized by President Mirabeau Buonaparte Lamar of Texas, to establish trade with New Mexico was met by Governor Manuel Armijo's Mexican troops and ended disastrously. The

Above: Officer's Row at Fort Davis National Historic Site, Texas. Built in 1854 to protect travelers through west Texas, the fort was named for Jefferson Davis, then Secretary of War of the United States and later president of the Confederate States of America.
PHOTO BY GEORGE H. H. HUEY

first Texans to surrender were executed and the remaining men were sent as prisoners to Mexico City. New Mexico was not anxious to join forces with the Texans and rise against the Mexican government.

Even though treaties had been signed between the Texans and Mexico, relations between the two countries were continually strained. Texas established its own navy to keep ports in the Gulf of Mexico open for trade with the U.S. and Europe. The Texas Navy's initial four ships were less than successful, with one captured by the Mexican fleet, two sunk and the fourth seized by a shipyard for non-payment of repair bills.

During the presidency of Sam Houston, eight new ships were ordered, including the 600-ton, 130 foot, twenty gun *Austin*. The new ships were successful in raiding the Mexicans and were leased to rebel forces in Yucatán under an agreement with President Lamar, who succeeded Houston. After Texas was annexed by the U.S., all ships of the Texas Navy were then transferred to the U.S. Navy. Only the *Austin* was still fit for service.

Sloop-of-War *Austin* of the Texas Navy.

The conflict between Texas and Mexico was closely monitored by the United States, Great Britain and France. The Europeans attempted to pressure Mexico into formally honoring the treaties between Santa Anna and Texas to no avail. They hoped to keep Texas from becoming part of the United States and felt Mexican recognition would help the Texans feel more secure as an independent nation.

In February of 1845, the U.S. offered Texas statehood, which the Texans accepted in December of the same year. The annexation of Texas by the United States soon led to the Mexican War of 1846.

General Zachary Taylor was sent by President Polk to protect Texas in the summer of 1845. Taylor succeeded Polk as president in 1849.

Immediately upon annexation of Texas by the United States, diplomatic relations between the U.S. and Mexico were broken off by the Mexicans as disputes over southern Texas boundaries mushroomed. President James K. Polk sent John Slidell to Mexico City to attempt to negotiate a settlement with Mexico. Slidell

THE BUFFALO SOLDIERS

Following the Civil War, Fort Davis, Texas, and other army installations throughout the Southwest were manned by two cavalry regiments, the Ninth and Tenth, and four infantry regiments which were comprised of black soldiers who were former slaves freed at the war's end. These courageous soldiers, called buffalo soldiers by the Indians, were an important factor in the eventual control of hostile Indian tribes in the Southwest.

The buffalo soldiers were deployed against the Kiowas, Comanches, Apaches, Kickapoos, Lipans and Utes. They were also used in the construction of telegraph lines, and provided escort for wagon trains, stage coaches, trains, cattle drives and survey parties.

Above: Forage cap on bunk in the enlisted men's barracks at Fort Davis National Historic Site. Fort Davis was manned by the Buffalo Soldiers.
PHOTO BY GEORGE H. H. HUEY

The buffalo soldiers were involved in the last Apache battle fought in Texas, in 1880, which brought Apache raids along the border to an end. Buffalo soldiers from Fort Davis were transferred to Arizona in 1885, and aided in the campaign resulting in Geronimo's final surrender the following year.

The buffalo soldiers were among the bravest soldiers on the frontier, highly decorated, and included many Medal of Honor winners.

Left: Enlisted men's equipment hanging over a bunk at Fort Davis National Historic Site. Fort Davis was abandoned in 1891, having outlived its usefulness. Today, carefully reconstructed grounds give insight into the lives of the men who served at Fort Davis.
PHOTO BY GEORGE H. H. HUEY

was authorized to offer the Mexicans $25 million for Texas, New Mexico, Arizona, and California. Slidell was rebuked by the Mexicans.

President Polk sent General Zachary Taylor, "Old Rough and Ready," to Texas in the summer of 1845 to protect the Texans against Mexican intervention. Polk ordered Taylor to move his army south to the Rio Grande in January of 1846. He prepared a letter to Congress in May asking for a declaration of war against Mexico on the basis that Mexico had evaded its financial obligations and insulted the United States by rejecting Slidell's mission. Before the letter was sent, the Mexican Army crossed the Rio Grande and attacked U.S. troops. Polk amended his letter to read, "Mexico has passed the boundary of the United States and shed American blood upon American soil. War exists by act of Mexico herself." The U.S. Congress declared war on May 13, 1846.

In September of 1846, General Taylor's army captured Monterrey, a Mexican stronghold in the north. General Santa Anna returned from Cuban exile and became president of Mexico once again. He force marched his army to engage General Taylor at Buena Vista, an ill-conceived plan that greatly depleted his army, more from the forced marches and the chaotic retreat, than the actual battle itself.

Above: Ruins of the U.S. Army's cavalry barracks at Fort Bowie National Historic Site in Arizona. The site preserves the remains of two forts, the first built in 1862, used during campaigns against the Apache in the late 1800's.
PHOTO BY GEORGE H. H. HUEY

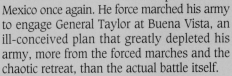

Colonel Stephen Kearny captured New Mexico in 1846 and protected the Santa Fe Trail.

Colonel Stephen Kearney, with nearly 1500 men in his Army of the West, was sent by Polk to New Mexico in the summer of 1846, where he was unopposed and easily captured the capital at Santa Fe without bloodshed. He proclaimed trader Charles Bent the first American governor of New Mexico. Leaving a force to guard Santa Fe, he sent part of his troops to Chihuahua to aid General Wool and set out personally with 300 men to California. On the trail he met a group of Americans, led by Kit Carson, who were heading to Washington with news that California had been taken by Colonel John C. Fremont and Navy Captain Robert Stockton of the United States.

Kit Carson, citizen of Taos and legendary mountain man, led Col. Kearny to California.

Kearny sent 200 of his men back to Santa Fe and was able to convince Carson to be his guide to California.

By the autumn of 1846, the United States accomplished its original goals and control of northeastern Mexico, New Mexico, Texas and California was in American hands.

General Winfield Scott, the commanding general of the United States Army, was sent to Mexico by President Polk to attempt to coerce peace and to establish control over additional Mexican territory. While the war had seemed to have ended, its major battles were yet to come. General Santa Anna used the lull in action to reinforce his army.

Scott's 11,000-man army included many of the officers who later commanded both Union and Confederate forces in the Civil War.

Captain Robert E. Lee was Scott's right hand, Ulysses S. Grant a quartermaster, P.G.T. Beauregard an aide, and Thomas J. "Stonewall" Jackson was a lieutenant. Future president Franklin Pierce enlisted as a private and became a general.

Robert E. Lee, as a U.S. Army captain in the Mexican War.

The Americans, courageously led by some of the greatest military leaders of all time, were able to drive their forces, at a great cost to the 30,000-man Mexican Army, to Mexico City and a negotiated peace with the signing of the treaty of Guadalupe Hidalgo in 1848.

Below: Wall of Mechanic's Corral at Fort Union National Monument. Fort Union was founded in 1851 for protection against Indian attacks.
PHOTO BY GEORGE H. H. HUEY

Anglo Settlement of the Southwest...

As the Mexican War came to an end with the signing of the Treaty of Guadalupe Hidalgo in 1848, American settlers began to immigrate to the Southwest in response to the low-cost land available. The population of Texas alone tripled to more than 600,000 between 1850 and 1860. The discovery of gold in California, in 1849, brought endless waves of immigrants through the Southwest, seeking to avoid the snow covered mountains of the northern routes by what they envisioned was an easier route through the Southwest.

The real advantages of the southern routes were slight, if they existed at all. In order to avoid the harsh winters in the mountains, the settlers faced searing desert heat, extremely limited water supplies, and the constant danger of attack by Comanche and Apache Indians, who were determined to keep the immigrants from encroaching upon their lands.

The U.S. Army remained in the Southwest following the Mexican War and began to finally bring the Indian uprisings under some semblance of control. Forts were built across the territory to offer protection to the settlers and travelers crossing the region. Fort Union in northern New Mexico was built by Colonel Edwin Sumner, and his troops, in 1851, three years after the end of the Mexican War. A second, semi-subterranean, earthworks Fort Union was constructed and reinforced with a battalion of Colorado volunteers during the Civil War, when many of the fort's officers left to join the ranks of the Confederacy. Although a confrontation between the Union fort and Confederate troops was expected, it never materialized. Fort Union, New Mexico, and the rest of the Southwest saw no major battles during the Civil War and were spared the bloodshed and devastation that destroyed the South. The third Fort Union, which became one of the Southwest's largest forts, served as a

Above: The ghost town of Chloride, New Mexico. Mining activity was the nucleus for many of the Southwestern towns established in the 1800's. When the mines played out, the towns often died.
PHOTO BY TOM TILL

supply post for the West following the Civil War and was used against raiding Indians until 1875. The fort was abandoned in 1891.

Fort Davis was built by the army in 1854, near the Apache Mountains in west Texas, to protect water sources and safeguard travelers. It became a Confederate fort when Texas seceded from the Union, but was abandoned by the Confederate Army in 1862 after they failed to take New Mexico. Following the Civil War, the U.S. Army reoccupied the fort. Fort Davis was home to the "buffalo soldiers," troops of emancipated blacks, who proved courageous and successful in the Indian Wars. After the final surrender of the Apaches in 1886, the fort was only used for another five years before being abandoned.

In 1862, Fort Bowie was built in southern Arizona by a group of Union volunteers, commanded by Brigadier General James H. Carleton, to protect the Arizona Territory from any Confederate intrusions, which never occurred. The fort successfully resisted Indian threats during the war and was replaced, in 1868, by a second Fort Bowie in a better location. Fort Bowie was used in campaigns to bring the Apache under control. After the final capture of Geronimo, the fort had outlived its usefulness and was officially abandoned in 1894.

As settlers, miners and ranchers poured into the Southwest following the Civil War, confrontations with the Indians continued until they were overwhelmed by the superior weaponry and the sheer number of Americans. The railroads began to criss-cross the land, making travel from the east to the frontier safe from Indian harassment, and bringing additional waves of American immigrants into the rapidly expanding Southwest.

The Union Pacific Railroad, which became the first railroad line to cross the continent in 1869, completed its link from Omaha, Nebraska, to the midsection of the Great Plains in 1867. This proved a major stimulus to the Texas cattle industry. A second line, the Atchison, Topeka and Santa Fe, cut through the territory in 1868 and gave ranchers a link with St. Louis, Missouri. The Eastern markets were clamoring for good quality beef following the Civil War, and in Texas cattle were roaming free on the range. By 1865, there were more than five million head of cattle in Texas, far more than the local markets could absorb.

In 1866, Texas ranchers herded more than 250,000 head of cattle to Sedalia, Missouri, in a combined effort to reach the markets in the East. Although the country was crawling with outlaws, who had entered the territory

Left: Cattle drive through Cumbres Pass in the Rio Grande National Forest, Colorado. The great cattle drives of the late 1800's supplied eastern markets with much sought after beef and stimulated the economy of the Southwest.
PHOTO BY TOM BEAN

in the relatively lawless years following the end of the Civil War, a majority of the herd reached its final destination and proved that cattle could be herded long distances, grazing along the way, and still arrive in a marketable condition. Special rail facilities and holding pens were constructed to handle the cattle in Abilene, Kansas, which became known as the railhead of the cattle kingdom. Between 1867 and 1871, cattlemen drove 1,460,000 head to Abilene along the Chisholm Trail.

Not all cattle drives were bound for Eastern markets. In 1866, Charles Goodnight and Oliver Loving gathered about 2,000 steers and herded them southwest. At Fort Sumner, New Mexico, they sold 1,200 head to the army and Goodnight returned to Texas to get more cattle. Loving continued on to Denver, where he sold the balance of the herd to John Wesley Iliff, who had a contract to supply beef to the Union Pacific Railroad's track laying crews. Their route became known as the Goodnight-Loving Trail.

The cattle boom led to leasing grasslands and contracts for raising corn from settlers, and in many cases Indian tribes, to fatten the cattle on their way to market. The Texas cattle kingdom was so immense that although five million head were sent to market by 1880, almost six million head were still on hand. Richard King, perhaps the greatest of the Texas ranchers, owned a 600,000 acre empire that delivered as many as 60,000 head a year to the markets in Kansas.

The invention of barbed wire by Joseph F. Glidden, in 1874, brought an end to open range grazing and started wars between rival factions claiming the same territory. These wars were often staffed on both sides by professional gunmen who ruthlessly obeyed only the laws of their employers. With the prosperity of the cattle boom also came rustlers stealing the herds of others and frontier towns offering whiskey, women and gambling as diversions for the cowboys at the end of the cattle drive.

The Southwest experienced a period of both prosperity and lawlessness that was unrivaled in the United States following the Civil War. Often, lawmen were no more than outlaws with a badge and in many towns the law was controlled by the most powerful business interests. It was not until around the beginning of the 20th Century that law and order was permanently established in the Southwest.

Below: Pipe Spring National Monument, near the border of Arizona and Utah, was established in 1858 by Mormon missionary Jacob Hamblin. It was later used by Brigham Young as a location for the Mormon Church's cattle herd.
PHOTO BY GEORGE H. H. HUEY

LAW AND ORDER IN THE SOUTHWEST...

In the Southwest there was often a very thin line between the good guys and the bad. Control of frontier towns was often held by gamblers and gunmen, some who wore a badge. As mining and cattle ranching brought new riches into the Southwest, and cowboys' and miners' pockets were filled with wages, a sinister element arose to separate men from their money, and often their lives.

Saloons offered whiskey, gambling and women for recreation. Professional gamblers turned games of chance into fleecings. Tempers flared and working men died at the hands of the gamblers. Outlaws robbed banks, trains and stage–coaches regularly. Some men were as quick to murder others in a gun fight as they were to jump their claims or to steal their cattle. The man with the fastest six-gun was often a law unto himself.

Tombstone Marshal Wyatt Earp was a lawman, gambler and gunfighter.

The story of Wyatt Earp and Doc Holliday illustrates the thin line between the good guys and the bad. Wyatt began his controversial career in law enforcement in 1870, when he was elected as a constable in Lamar, Missouri. He resigned less than a year later and drifted south to Oklahoma, where he and two friends stole horses belonging to William Keys.

Earp and his companions were captured by a posse led by James Keys, William's brother,

and placed under citizen's arrest. They were transported to Van Buren, Arkansas, where they faced charges as horse thieves. After posting a $500 bail, Wyatt fled the territory.

Above: The Tombstone Epitaph office in Tombstone, Arizona. The newspaper, founded in 1880, reported the famous gunfight at the OK Corral between the Earp and Clanton factions.
PHOTO BY DICK DIETRICH

By 1874, he was making a living as a gambler in Wichita, Kansas, where his brother, James, was tending bar. Jim's wife ran a bordello where Kate Elder, later Doc Holliday's mistress, was employed. Wyatt was elected as a city policeman in Wichita's 1875 municipal election. When not involved with his official duties, he gambled and collected protection money

from saloon keepers. Wyatt was fired when officials learned of his extortion racket, so he left town and followed the gambling circuit to Dodge City, where he once again became a law enforcement officer.

Famous lawman, gambler and gunfighter Bat Masterson was a close friend of Wyatt. He met John Henry "Doc" Holliday, a dentist and a professional gambler, in late 1877. A strong bond formed between these men that was summed up by a quote from Bat Masterson: "Doc's whole heart and soul

John Henry "Doc" Holliday, dentist and gunfighter.

were wrapped up in Wyatt Earp and he was always ready to stake his life in defense of any cause in which Wyatt was interested." The two men would remain extremely close until Holliday's death from tuberculosis in 1887.

While a lawman in Dodge City, Wyatt again collected protection money. He owned interests in the Long Branch Saloon and the Alhambra Saloon. His only Dodge City gunfight resulting in death was in July of 1878. George Hoyt, a cowboy on bail pending charges of cattle rustling, got into a drunken argument with a theater owner. He rode by the rear of the theater, firing shots at the building. As he rode away, Wyatt and Jim Masterson, Bat's brother, engaged him in a gunfight and took his life.

Bat Masterson was an Earp associate, gunfighter, lawman and later a reporter for a New York City newspaper.

Wyatt was rescued by Sheriff Bat Masterson when three rowdy Missourians attempted to assassinate him. The same gunmen later tried to kill Masterson, who was tipped off by a friend. It is believed that two of the men may have been the famous outlaws, Frank and Jesse James.

In 1879, Wyatt traveled to Las Vegas, New Mexico, via a stop in Mobeetie, Texas, with gambler friend "Mysterious Dave" Mather. The two men were run out of Texas by the notoriously tough lawman, James McIntire, for swindling cowboys in a "gold brick" hoax. By the time Wyatt and his brothers, Jim, Morgan and Virgil, arrived in Tombstone, Arizona, they were

"Mysterious Dave" Mather, outlaw and lawman, ran a fake gold brick scam in Mobeetie, Texas, with Wyatt Earp.

THE GUNFIGHT AT THE O.K. CORRAL

The Earp faction, Wyatt, Virgil, and Morgan Earp, along with their longtime friend, Doc Holliday, had long feuded with the Clanton-McLaury faction. Each accused the other of stage-coach robberies and murder. The evidence pointed to the Earps and Holliday. Tensions mounted until they reached a boiling point.

On October 25, 1881, Wyatt, Morgan and Doc Holliday cornered Ike Clanton and tried several times to incite him into a gunfight. Clanton was unarmed and left to get his gun. He returned and told Wyatt to be ready for a showdown in the morning. The next morning Virgil, the only Earp still a "lawman," pistol-whipped Ike and arrested him for carrying a gun within city limits. He was taken to court and fined $25. Tom McLaury came to the courthouse to aid Ike. As they left, Tom collided with Wyatt on the sidewalk, and Wyatt pistol-whipped McLaury for the accident.

At 2:30, the Earps and Holliday decided to gun down the Clantons and McLaurys. Sheriff John Behan attempted to calm the hostilities but was told by Virgil, "I will not arrest them, but will kill them on sight." The Earp-Holliday faction found Ike and Billy Clanton, Tom and Frank McLaury, and Billy Claiborne standing in a lot near the O.K. Corral, but not in the corral as legend has it.

Virgil told the men to throw up their hands, causing them to reach for their guns. Claiborne

broke and ran, handing his pistol to the unarmed Tom McLaury. Virgil shot Claiborne anyway. Frank McLaury was shot in the stomach and fatally wounded by Wyatt's first bullet. Holliday shot Tom McLaury in the chest and side with a sawed-off shotgun. Ike Clanton grabbed Wyatt's gun hand, pinned him against a wall, then threw him to the ground and ran inside a boarding house. Morgan shot Billy Clanton in the chest and Virgil shot him in the stomach. As Billy Clanton lay dying, he wounded Morgan in the neck and shoulder and Virgil in the leg.

In less than a minute the gunfight was over. Sheriff Behan tried to arrest Wyatt, who refused to be arrested. The three dead men, Billy Clanton, Tom McLaury, and Frank McLaury, were dressed in fine clothes and displayed in a store window with a sign stating, "murdered in the streets of Tombstone." They were buried on Boot Hill.

Tom and Frank McLaury, with Billy Clanton, on display in a hardware store window.

already notorious throughout the Southwest.

In 1880, Virgil Earp was appointed assistant marshal of Tombstone. Wyatt was dismissed from a similar position and was replaced by John H. Behan. Wyatt and Behan became bitter enemies, their feud further increasing when Behan's young mistress, Josephine Sarah Marcus, left him for Wyatt.

Marshal Virgil Earp.

Wyatt bought an interest in the Oriental Saloon and hired his brother Morgan, Doc Holliday, Luke Short, and Bat Masterson as dealers. The Earps were soon back to their old patterns of gambling and brawling. During this time it was charged that Doc Holliday, who had already killed several men, and the Earps were responsible for several stage-coach robberies and a murder. The evidence pointed strongly to Doc Holliday, including reports from eye-witnesses and a sworn statement from Doc Holliday's mistress, Kate Elder. The person bringing

Cattle rancher Ike Clanton was also a cattle rustler.

these charges was rancher Ike Clanton who, along with his brother Billy and their friends Frank and Tom McLaury, was a known cattle rustler. Clanton testified against the Earp faction during a preliminary hearing. Wyatt countered, without a shred of evidence, that the robberies and murder were committed by Ike and Billy Clanton and Frank and Tom McLaury. As the accusations flew, the stage was set for the most famous gunfight in history...The Gunfight at the O.K. Corral (see sidebar on opposite page).

Not all bad men crossed the line between serving the law and breaking it. Plenty of them were just plain bad, and some were crazy. Clay Allison was an excellent example of the latter. Discharged from the army as "partly epileptic and party maniacal," he killed a man accused of several murders, cut off his head and impaled it on a stick, which he carried twenty miles to show off in a saloon. He was invited to dinner by an outlaw named Chunk Colbert, after which he shot him in the head. When asked why he had accepted the man's dinner invitation if he had meant to kill him, Allison replied, "I didn't want to send a man to hell on an empty stomach." A dentist once drilled one of Allison's teeth in error. Allison pinned the

Morgan Earp was killed by four men, who shot him in the back, within a few months of the famous gunfight at the O.K. Corral.

dentist to a chair and pulled one of his teeth and was working on a second when the man's screams brought help and stopped the operation.

Allison died bringing a wagonload of supplies to his ranch from Pecos, Texas. A sack of grain fell and as Allison reached for it he fell from the wagon. His neck was broken by the wagon's wheel.

Clay Allison was a crazed gunman. He often killed with a bizarre twist.

The most famous Texas outlaw was John Wesley Hardin, who claimed to have killed 44 men. He stabbed his first victim as a young schoolboy. At fifteen, he killed a black man who came at him with a stick. When three soldiers came to question him about the murder, he ambushed and killed them. Hardin killed six Mexicans while working a cattle drive from southern Texas to Abilene, Kansas.

John Wesley Hardin killed 44 men, four before he turned 16. His was thought to be the fastest draw in the West.

While in Abilene, Hardin met Wild Bill Hickok, who was the town's leading peace officer. The two men formed a strange bond, with Hardin fascinated by Wild Bill, who he knew would kill him without a second thought if the need arose. While staying at a hotel, he killed a man for snoring. Fearing Wild Bill Hickok, he fled to Texas and never again set foot in Kansas.

Back in Texas, Hardin killed deputy sheriff Charles Webb, who had tried to shoot Hardin in the back but failed when a warning was shouted. Webb was Hardin's 39th victim.

He fled to Florida where he lived under an alias for two years. Invited to join local police in hunting a group of criminals, Hardin killed his only man in the name of the law. He left Florida and headed toward Mexico, killing two lawmen who tried to apprehend him. He killed his 43rd and 44th victims over a poker game in Alabama.

On July 23, 1877, Hardin

"Wild Bill" Hickok, the famous lawman and gunfighter, was the only man that John Wesley Hardin ever feared.

was cornered on a train at Pensacola Junction, Florida, by Texas Ranger John Armstrong and a group of local deputies. Sent to Huntsville Prison for the earlier killing of deputy sheriff Webb, Hardin spent 15 years in prison. The Webb shooting was, ironically, probably his most righteous shooting. In prison, he studied law which he practiced after his pardon in 1894. He was killed July 19, 1895 in El Paso, Texas when policeman John Selman shot him in the back of the head over an argument.

Below: Capitol Reef National Park, Utah. Outlaws Butch Cassidy and the Sundance Kid visited the area and bought supplies from Mormon settlers. PHOTO BY TOM TILL

William H. Bonney, better known as Billy the Kid, claimed to have killed 21 men before his 21st birthday. Born in New York City, he moved to New Mexico when his mother remarried in 1873. His father had died at the end of the Civil War and his mother died from illness in 1874. Billy was 14 years old. He was well liked by his teachers, who said he was no more a problem than any other boy, and his first boss said that Billy was "the only kid who ever worked here and never stole anything."

Billy's first scrape with the law came at the tender age of fifteen. Another youth playing a joke on a Chinese laundryman stole a bundle of clothes and had Billy hide them. He was caught by the local police who decided to teach him a lesson by placing him in jail. Terrified at being in confinement, he escaped after two days by climbing up a chimney. He then drifted west to Camp Grant, Arizona.

Billy the Kid killed 21 men before his 21st birthday. He was killed before he reached 22 by his friend, Sheriff Pat Garrett.

It was at Camp Grant that the Kid killed his first man. Frank Cahill, a burly blacksmith, enjoyed teasing the Kid. Cahill called Billy a pimp, a highly unlikely charge, and Billy called Cahill a "sonofabitch." The blacksmith slapped his face and threw him to the floor. Billy, no match for Cahill in a fist-fight, drew his revolver and shot him. Cahill died the following day and Billy the Kid was once again confined to jail.

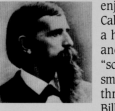

Lew Wallace, the governor of New Mexico, offered a pardon to Billy the Kid in return for testimony against participants in the bloody Lincoln County War.

The Kid escaped again and made his way back to New Mexico, where he was involved in the Lincoln County War. He became a cattle guard for John Tunstall, an Englishman, who Billy greatly admired. When Tunstall was murdered by members of a rival faction, Billy vowed to avenge his death and killed several men in retaliation. After John Tunstall's death something inside Billy snapped and he became a ruthless killer. Ambushing, back-shooting, and shooting men who were unarmed was not beneath the Kid.

New Mexico Governor Lew Wallace, a retired army general who later wrote the classic novel *Ben Hur*, offered Billy a complete pardon if he would testify against others involved in murders during the Lincoln County War. The Kid testified, actually enjoying himself as he did so, but rode off before he stood trial for the murders he had committed, and therefore remained unpardoned. Governor Wallace was furious that the Kid broke his word after he had personally arranged for a second chance for Billy. He assigned Billy's one-time friend, Pat Garrett, the Sheriff of Lincoln County, the difficult task of bringing Billy the Kid in to face murder charges. Garrett formed a posse and caught up with the Kid and his men at a ranch in Stinking Springs. He held the outlaws under siege in a farm–house for two days before Billy and his men surrendered. The Kid was taken to Santa Fe.

Billy went to trial and was found guilty of the murder of Andrew Roberts. He was sentenced to hang and was escorted back to Lincoln by two of Garrett's deputies, J.W. Bell and Robert Ollinger. Ollinger, who had been part of a rival faction in the Lincoln County War, did not try to hide his dislike for the Kid. He prodded Billy with the barrel of his shotgun whenever the Kid had to go to the bathroom and begged him to run so he could shoot Billy in the back–the way, he said, the Kid had shot his friends.

Bell told Ollinger to leave the Kid alone on several occasions and always treated Billy

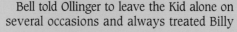

Sheriff Pat Garrett was a friend to Billy the Kid, but later shot him to death in a dark room.

with kindness. On April 28, 1881, Billy asked Bell to take him to the bathroom. Hobbling in leg irons, Billy knocked Bell down and jumped into Garrett's gun room. He grabbed a pistol as Bell came running into the room. Bell pleaded with the Kid to put down the gun, but all Billy said was, "Sorry Bell," and shot him dead. Billy went to the stairs and waited for Ollinger, who he knew would come running at the sound of the shot. When Ollinger arrived, the Kid said in a friendly voice, "Hello Bob," and let loose with a double barrel shotgun that almost completely blew Ollinger's head off.

Garrett pursued Billy across New Mexico for three months before he tracked him down at the Maxwell ranch. When Billy heard noises in the

Bob Ollinger made a fatal mistake when he tormented Billy the Kid while he was in jail. The Kid shot him in the head with both barrels of a shotgun as he escaped.

night, he went outside to investigate. Garrett snuck into a darkened bedroom and waited for his return. When the Kid came in saying, "Quien es?...Quien es?," Garrett shot him through the heart. Billy the Kid was just months shy of his twenty-second birthday.

Below: The ruins of the Dragoon Springs Station of the Butterfield Stage Lines. Stage-coaches were considered easy targets by outlaws.
PHOTO BY JACK W. DYKINGA

Texan Bill Longley was responsible for 32 murders by the time he was 27. He killed his first man, a black lawman, at the age of fifteen. When he was finally caught and convicted of murder for killing a man who had shot his cousin, he was sentenced to be hung. Well known for his bravado, he wrote to a girl, "Hanging is my favorite way of dying." While on the gallows he surveyed the crowd of 4,000 who had gathered to witness his execution and said, "I see a good many enemies around, and mighty few friends."

Bill Longley was the murderer of 32 men by the age of 27.

Not all outlaws were unpopular; many became folk heroes from glamorized accounts in newspapers and books. Most were murderers without any redeeming qualities. An exception to this rule was Robert LeRoy Parker, better known as Butch Cassidy. Born in Utah, Butch was the grandson of a Mormon bishop and was always against using murder in his bank and train robberies.

His gang, the Wild Bunch, consisted of Harry Longbaugh, the "Sundance Kid," a well-known fast-draw artist; Will "News" Carver; Harvey Logan, also known as "Kid Curry;" and Ben Kilpatrick, the "Tall Texan." They were the last of the Old West bank and train robbers.

Above: Butch Cassidy, seated right, the Sundance Kid, seated left, and the Wild Bunch.

Above: Cell blocks at the Yuma Territorial Prison, Yuma, Arizona. Built in 1876, these walls were home to 3,040 men and 29 women before the prison closed in 1909.
PHOTO BY JEFF GNASS

The gang's hideout was at Hole-in-the-Wall in Colorado, although they traveled the country and lived the high life. Events heated up after the gang robbed a Union Pacific Railroad train on June 2, 1899. They tried to persuade a guard in the express car, a man named Woodcock, to open the door. When he refused, dynamite was used to blow the door open. Woodcock was injured but alive. Kid Currey wanted to shoot Woodcock but Butch intervened saying, "Now Harvey, a man with that kind of nerve deserves not to be shot." The Union Pacific Railroad hired the Pinkerton Detective Agency to track down the gang. Posses were formed and led by famous lawmen N.K. Boswell, Joe Lefors and Charles Siringo who were hired by Pinkerton to capture the gang.

Butch Cassidy was proud of the fact he never killed a man.

The Wild Bunch robbed yet another Union Pacific train, and Woodcock was once again the guard. This time he opened the door and the gang made off with $50,000.

The Pinkerton pursuit intensified and Butch, the Sundance Kid and Etta Place, the Kid's woman, moved to South America and continued their crime spree. Some say South American troops killed the outlaws, and others say they quietly lived out their lives back home.

The Sundance Kid and Etta Place in New York City.

Following Pages: Durango & Silverton Narrow Gauge Railroad in Colorado's San Juan Mountains.
PHOTO BY TOM TILL

THE LEGEND OF THE LOST DUTCHMAN'S MINE

A frenzied whisper of "gold" spread through the camp like wildfire on a parched summer day as Adolph Ruth wandered onto the Quarter Circle U Ranch, which was owned and operated by Tex Barkley. Ruth had maps, old and very mysterious, said to have been penned by Jacob Waltz, the legendary, if not accurately named, Lost Dutchman. Supposedly, somewhere in the mountains adjacent to Barkley's ranch, was the famed Lost Dutchman's Mine and Ruth wanted Barkley's help to find the spot near the "pointed peak" in the heart of the Superstition Mountains, where the maps indicated the mine's location.

Barkley sighed and scratched his grizzled chin. This fortune hunter from back east was easily in his early sixties, and not in the best of shape. How would he ever survive the rugged trip into the Superstition Wilderness, let alone in the dead of summer? The heat was so scorching that even the nastiest rattlesnakes knew better than to venture out into the sun. But the old man was so anxious, Barkley feared, that he may be crazy enough to strike out on his own. Barkley agreed to take Ruth, but Ruth was too impatient to wait three days until Barkley could make the trip to Phoenix for supplies.

With two cowboy guides, Adolph Ruth set off in search of the Lost Dutchman's Mine without Barkley. That was the last time Tex Barkley saw Ruth alive. When he returned to his ranch and discovered Ruth gone, Barkley saddled up and took off looking for him, fearing the worst–for Ruth had talked too much and to too many people about his treasured maps, which he always kept close to his heart in a shirt breast pocket. Too many people have gold fever, thought Tex Barkley, and too many men would kill for a chance at the rumored riches of Jacob Waltz' Lost Dutchman's Mine.

Well into August the search continued for Adolph Ruth, as ranchers and sheriff's deputies spent long days in the blistering sun combing the area on horseback. They concentrated on the area around a peak called "Weaver's Needle," looking for a trace of the prospector's whereabouts, or his remains. Days stretched into weeks and still no trace of Adolph Ruth was found. After forty-five days, the searchers gave up in despair.

It wasn't until a chilly day in December that a ranchhand from the Quarter Circle U made a grisly find on a trek into the forbidding Superstitions. The partially decomposed skull turned out to be that of Adolph Ruth. Some claim there were bullet holes in the skull...others say he died of

Prickly pear and saguaro cactus beneath rock pinnacles in the Superstition Mountains. One of the pinnacles in the area is alleged to be a key to the location of the Lost Dutchman's Mine.
PHOTO BY CARR CLIFTON

natural causes. One thing was sure, Adolph Ruth was dead, a casualty of the lure of the Lost Dutchman's Mine and its hidden gold. It has been said that gold, like war, brings out the best and the worst in a man. Adolph Ruth died as another testimony to that fact.

THE NATIVE AMERICANS

The Indians of the Southwest are direct ancestors of nomadic tribes that crossed the Bering Straits during the long period of glaciation that ended concurrently with the ending of the Pleistocene Epoch, or Ice Age, more than eleven thousand years ago. They arrived at different times, and are undoubtedly from several different original groups. The major tribes of historic times are related in part to the prehistoric Pueblo cultures, Plains Indians, and Athabascan nomadic tribes from Canada in the north.

Southwestern Indian tribes of historic times include Acoma, Apache, Caddo, Chemehuevi, Cochiti, Cocopah, Comanche, Havasupai, Hopi, Hualapai, Isleta, Jemez, Kiowa, Laguna, Mohave, Maricopa, Nambre, Navajo, Paiute, Picuris, Pima, Pojaque, San Felipe, San Ildefonso, San Juan, Sandia, Santa Ana, Santa Clara, Santo Domingo, Taos, Tesque, Tohono O'otam, Ute, Yavapai, Yaqui, Yuma, Zia, and Zuñi.

The fiercely independent Navajo, who had an uneasy relationship with the Europeans and many of their Indian neighbors in both prehistoric and historic times, are the largest of all Native American tribes. The Navajo Indian Reservation covers a vast territory, around 16 million acres of land, that includes portions of Arizona, Utah and New Mexico, and is home to around 160,000 Navajos.

The Navajo were Athabascans who migrated into the Southwest from Canada several centuries before the arrival of the Spaniards. A nomadic hunter-gatherer people, the Navajo are closely related to the Apache, and chose the region of their current reservation as their homeland. Prior to the arrival of the Spanish, the Navajo conducted frequent raids against the Pueblo Indians and their other neighbors. The Utes made continual efforts to force the Navajo from northern New Mexico but were less than successful.

The Navajo often chose the intricate canyons of Canyon de Chelly as a refuge from intruders and pursuers seeking retaliation for their raids. The entire area was fortress-like in its natural state. By 1805, the Spanish had reached the end of their patience with the Navajo who, like the Comanche and Apache, had proven much harder to control than the semi-peaceful Pueblo Indians. A Spanish detachment, under the leadership of Lt. Colonel Antonio Narbona, was sent by the governor of New Mexico to put an end to the Navajo raiding.

After a lengthy pursuit the Spanish engaged the Navajo at Canyon del Muerto, in Canyon de Chelly. In a day-long battle, Navajo warriors, women, and children took shelter in a cave, now aptly called Massacre Cave, near the top of the canyon. The Spanish forces fired on the warriors, and defenseless Indian women and children, from a point on the canyon rim above. When the slaughter was over, more than 100 Indians, mostly women and children, were dead. Narbona, in his official report to the governor in Santa Fe, had an entirely different account of the confrontation.

Narbona stated that 115 Navajo were killed, including 90 warriors, and that 33 were taken prisoner. No mention was made of the women and children, probably a wise decision on Narbona's part since the Spanish Crown did

With the arrival of the first Europeans in the Southwest, the Spanish conquistadors, came the decline of the Native American populations and influence. The Pueblo Indians alternately attempted to exist peacefully with the less than gracious intruders, then expelled them in the 1680 Pueblo Revolt. The nomadic bands were slightly more successful, with Comanches, Apaches, Navajos and Utes continuing to raid both Pueblo Indians and the white settlers until the Anglo-Americans arrived. The Anglo-Americans had less influence over the Pueblo Indians than the Spaniards, but were entirely successful in eliminating the threat of the hostile raiders.

Left: Spider Rock in Canyon de Chelly National Monument. The intricate canyons of Canyon de Chelly were used by the Navajo for protection from intruders and pursuers for hundreds of years. The Navajo, who jointly operate Canyon de Chelly with the National Park Service, still live in the area and raise crops in the canyon.
PHOTO BY JERRY JACKA

Right: Navajo pictographs of Spanish horsemen in Blue Bull Cave at Canyon del Muerto in Canyon de Chelly National Monument.
PHOTO BY GEORGE H. H. HUEY

not seek the genocide of their Indian subjects. Colonel Narbona later substantiated his claims with a package that contained the ears of 84 Indians, with an apology for the missing pairs. The captives were enslaved by the Spaniards. The loss of life to the Spanish troops in the one-sided encounter was limited to a single man who fell from the cliff to the canyon floor.

The Navajo had learned the ineffectiveness of arrows and stones against the rifles of the white man, and kept a relatively low profile throughout the remaining years of Spanish influence. The Navajo, like the Apache, had always lead an existence supplemented by raids on other tribes, and now, on the foreign intruders. When the area passed from Spanish and Mexican control, to the Americans in 1848, the Navajo found themselves once again at odds with the white man.

Increased Navajo raiding against American settlers, who were encroaching on Navajo tribal lands, soon caused the white settlers to call for retaliation. In 1863, the U.S. Army, under the command of Brigadier General James

Henry Carleton, sent Christopher "Kit" Carson, the former mountain man and Indian scout, north with orders to engage the Navajo. Carson, who was commissioned a Colonel of the volunteers, was ordered by the ruthless Carleton: "All Indian men of that tribe are to be killed whenever and wherever you find them; the women and children will not be harmed, but you will take them prisoners." Carson's orders were clear; he was not to make any attempt at peace but to kill the Navajo men in their entirety.

In the summer of 1863, Carson gathered 736 volunteers consisting of Spanish and American settlers, Utes, Zuñi, and some Hopi Indians–all unsympathetic to the Navajo–and set out to systematically complete this task. On route to Canyon de Chelly, Carson and his volunteers burned Navajo houses, killed their sheep, and destroyed their fields. His attacks were so effective that, by September, large numbers of Navajos began to surrender. Many sought refuge at Fort Defiance, where they were given food and protection. Bands of

Navajos fled in all directions. Some joined with other tribes and others took refuge in remote areas to the north. By January of 1864, the only Navajos that were still at large were hiding in the Canyon de Chelly area.

When Kit Carson arrived at the mouth of Canyon de Chelly in January of 1864, he knew the battle was all but won. The Navajos had long used the canyon area as a summer home, but were not equipped to survive in the area in winter. Carson, to his credit, sent dispatches to General Carleton arguing that there were too few Indians left in the canyon to justify the hardships his troops would face during a harsh winter campaign. Carleton, unfortunately for the remaining Navajos, felt a decisive victory would achieve a lasting psychological effect on Navajos everywhere, and ordered Carson to proceed into the Canyon.

By April of 1864, cold and hunger forced the final surrender of the Navajos in Canyon de Chelly. More than 8,000 Navajo men, women and children began what then became known as the "Long Walk" to their place of exile at Fort Sumner, New Mexico. Bosque Redondo, the new reservation, was a treeless and barren land where many thousands of Navajos later died due to exposure to the elements and the white man's diseases. After four years, the United States Army acknowledged their error in judgement and let the Navajos return to the location of their present reservation.

The four years the Navajos spent at Bosque Redondo were a sad and particularly painful time. Fortunately, the Navajos are a bright and enterprising people. They used their years of confinement to learn from other captives, and their captors, as much as they could about the changing times and the world they were forced into. It was during these years of confinement that the Navajos learned the art of jewelry making for which they are now famous.

The Hopi Indians, abbreviated from Hopituh Shi-nu-mu, which means "the peaceful people," are the only remaining pueblo dwellers in Arizona. The Hopi have occupied their domain

Left: A view from the rim into Canyon del Muerto, Canyon de Chelly National Monument. In 1805, Spanish soldiers engaged the Navajos at Canyon del Muerto in a day-long battle. The Navajo men, women and children took shelter in a cave, now called Massacre Cave, near the top of the canyon. The Spaniards fired upon the Indians from the rim above, beyond the range of the Indians' weapons. When the battle was over, more than 100 Navajos had died at the cost of a single Spaniard, who fell from the rim into the canyon below.
PHOTO BY LARRY ULRICH

Right: Cochise Head looms above spires of rhyolite and Arizona cypress trees at Chiricahua National Monument. The Chiricahua Apache lived in these canyons for centuries, until encroachment by the early American settlers drove them from the area in the late 1880's.
PHOTO BY TOM DANIELSEN

for hundreds of years, in villages on top the high, barren mesas in northern Arizona.

Thomas V. Keam, an Englishman, started a trading post in 1878, near the three Hopi mesas in an area that came to be known as Keams Canyon. Keams named the mesas "First Mesa," "Second Mesa," and "Third Mesa," opposite of the order the Hopi referred to their ancestral sites. In ancient times, these mesas, the three southern prongs of Black Mesa, provided the Hopi Indians with natural protection from their enemies.

In 1543, Spaniards, under the command of Don Pedro de Tovar, first visited the Hopi. They brought gifts and established a camp near Kawaiokuh, which today is a ruin. From the Hopi, the Spaniards learned of the Colorado River and the Grand Canyon. Don Pedro de Tovar ordered Captain Garcia de Cardenas north to search for the Canyon and the river. The Spanish were unimpressed by the region, and its lack of precious minerals. They did not visit the Hopi again for another 40 years. When they returned, they attempted to convert the Hopi to Christianity, which they continued to do until the Hopi joined the other Pueblo Indians in the Pueblo Revolt of 1680. Spanish intervention meant little to the Hopi; they were not interested in the white man's God, and their remote and arid region did not attract white settlers.

Old Oraibi vies with the village of Acoma, in New Mexico, for the distinction of being the oldest continuously occupied village in North America. Both were established around 1100 A.D. Old Oraibi was one of the largest Hopi towns until 1906, when arguments over the education of Hopi children brought about

Above: Arches National Park. The Ute Indians occupied the Arches area long before the arrival of the first white men. In 1855, Mormons founded nearby Moab, but were prevented from settling the area by the Utes until the 1870's.
PHOTO BY JACK W. DYKINGA

the founding of Hotevilla, Bacabi, and New Oraibi on Third Mesa.

The Hopi have always been concerned with the preservation of their lands. For many centuries they have been completely surrounded by the Navajo, who were their traditional enemy. Through a series of treaties between the Navajo and Hopi, the federal government has attempted unsuccessfully to resolve their territorial conflicts on numerous occasions. Disputes over the ownership of these lands continue in Washington today.

The Hopi social organization is based upon the clan system, with strong ties to the mother. Homes are built adjacent to the mother's home, and men join their wife's clan upon marriage. Women own the houses, food, seeds for planting, the springs, wells and their gardens. Men do the hunting, farming, herding and yarn and leather work. An important aspect of the social structure is curing, which is under the control of medicine societies known as kachina. All Hopi are members of one of the numerous kachina cults.

The Hopi conduct many of their ceremonies to ensure the proper passage of the seasons, promote fertility in plants and animals, encourage rain, and to ensure hunting success. Many of these elaborate presentations are open to visitors. The Snake Dances are among the best known and most involved. Men and boys of the Snake and Antelope fraternities emerge from their kivas, painted and costumed, and search the surrounding countryside for four days

COCHISE, CHIRICAHUA APACHE LEGEND

Cochise, by the 1860's, was the tribal leader of the Tskanende Chiricahua Apache and known as a fearless warrior, and a shrewd strategist, by Indians, Mexicans and Americans alike. The son-in-law of famous Apache chief Mangus Coloradas, Cochise was a strong and compassionate leader. Although the Mexicans were terrified of him, he was considered to be a man of his word to all who knew him. At one time Cochise held contracts to deliver wood to the Butterfield Stagecoach station in Apache Pass, where he was well respected.

In early 1861, rancher John Ward reported the capture of his stepson, Felix Ward, by a band of Apaches. Although there was no evidence linking the abduction of the boy to Cochise and his band, a company of United States Army Infantry, led by a young Second Lieutenant, George Bascom, made contact with Cochise through an interpreter named Antonio. Cochise and several of his followers went to Bascom's camp for a parley.

Cochise and six of his followers entered a large tent with Lt. Bascom and several of his aides. In good faith, Cochise explained that he and his men had nothing to do with the missing boy, nor had they received any word of who the culprits may have been. As he spoke, Lt. Bascom's men were surrounding the tent. Bascom informed Cochise that he and his men were under arrest. With lightning fast reflexes, Cochise pulled his knife and

"You Americans began the fight, and now the Americans and Mexicans kill an Apache on sight. I have retaliated with all my might. I have killed ten white men for every Indian slain."

— Cochise

ripped through the rear of the tent, running at full speed toward freedom. The soldiers were caught completely unaware. By the time they regained their senses, and fired off more than 50 rounds, Cochise was out of range and unharmed.

The six Apache still in Bascom's tent were not able to escape and became Bascom's prisoners. The following day Cochise attempted to negotiate their release, as was the Apache custom in such situations. When Lt. Bascom refused to leave the security of his encampment, Cochise called to the Butterfield stationmaster, a stagecoach driver, and a hostler, who all knew and trusted him. Bascom refused to let the men go to talk with Cochise, but they started walking toward him anyway. Cochise made a move to grab the men, not intending to harm them but to trade them for his six warriors.

The stationmaster was seized by the Indians; the other two men panicked and ran. In the ensuing confusion, the Indians shot the stage driver, and the soldiers, believing the innkeeper to be an attacking Indian, shot him.

That evening Cochise and his band captured a small wagon train and took additional hostages. The next day Cochise, using the stationmaster as an interpreter, offered Bascom another trade, his hostages for Bascom's-plus Cochise would throw in sixteen government mules. Foolishly, Bascom refused unless the boy, who Cochise had never seen, was thrown in. As this charade continued over the next several days, Lt. Bascom continually received reinforcements. As Cochise gazed down on the scene from a hilltop vantage point, he knew the hostage trade talks were only a stalling tactic and he withdrew his band from the area.

The hostages were left behind, all murdered and shockingly mutilated. When Lt. Bascom and his troops arrived on the grisly scene, he ordered the six Apache, and three additional Coyotero captives, to be hung. Cochise, wrongly accused by Bascom of the kidnapping of young Felix Ward, was now on the warpath. The longer he contemplated the turn of events, the more furious he became.

Feeling there would never be equitable dealings with the white man, Cochise spent the next twenty years on the warpath exacting revenge.

gathering snakes. On the day of the Snake Dance, the Antelope priests line up in the plaza and await the arrival of the Snake priests. Upon the arrival of the Snake priests, gourds are rattled to emulate the sound of rattlesnakes, and the priests begin a deep sonorous chorus. As the chorus reaches a climax, the Snake men form groups of three and reach into a cottonwood bough, where a priest, who is hidden inside, hands them a snake. The snake is placed in the mouth of the Snake man, while his two assistants trail behind to control the snake. As many as 70 or 80 snakes may be involved in the ceremony. As the ceremony continues, Hopi women sprinkle corn meal on the snakes and the dancers. When all of the snakes are freed and placed within a circle, they dart in all directions. Pandemonium ensues among the Hopi and visitors alike, until all of the snakes have been collected. The Snake men then rush out of the village and down the trails to free the snakes. When the ceremony ends, the villagers relax and a four day festival begins.

Long before the arrival of the first Europeans, the Apache Indians, nomadic Athabascan bands, occupied the Southwest. Inhabiting an area from the eastern slopes of the Rocky Mountains, west to the base of the Sangre de Cristo Mountains (near Cimmaron and Las Vegas), and from the northern plains of the Colorado Plateau south to Texas and Mexico, Apaches led a simple existence. In the centuries prior to the arrival of the Spanish Franciscan priests, the Apaches were peaceful tribes that depended upon small and large game hunting, some simple farming, and the wild foods they gathered from the land.

Living in permanent villages, the Apaches conducted extensive bison hunts, grew maize and harvested great quantities of mescal. When it was necessary, they could literally "live off the land" by harvesting berries, roots, seeds and cactus, and by hunting game animals. The Apaches were extremely healthy and vigorous people before the introduction of the white man's diseases. They were capable of traveling

Above: Guadalupe Mountains National Park, Texas. The Apache occupied this region until they were overwhelmed by the United States Army, in 1886, and were removed to a reservation in the nearby Sacramento Mountains.
PHOTO BY CARR CLIFTON

great distances in the summer heat of the desert, and in the chilling cold of winter in the mountains, with little or no discomfort.

With the Apaches, past and present, women are held in high regard. They are protected, respected and cherished. Girls were given the

GERONIMO! APACHE GUERRILLA FIGHTER

Perhaps the most famous of all Apache warriors, Geronimo led the Bedonkohe Apache from their territory around the headwaters of the Gila River. Legendary for his bravery and tenacity, Geronimo was said, in numerous documented accounts, to have been clairvoyant. A story is told of Geronimo traveling home from a raid with a group of Mexican prisoners in tow, stopping, and suddenly saying to his band in a trance-like state, "Tomorrow afternoon, as we march back northward along the north side of the mountains, we will see a man standing on a hill to our left. He will howl to us and tell us that the troops have captured our base camp." The event occurred the next day just as Geronimo's vision predicted.

Geronimo was never able to fully understand the contradictory nature of the white man, who would seize Apache land with little regard for the Indians' rights. He wondered what gave these men the right to do this. Had their god given them these rights? The whites, Geronimo often mused, would plunder Apache lands, steal their horses, kill their people and destroy their villages. Why then did the white man think it was so strange when the Apache responded in like measure?

In May of 1883, Geronimo surrendered for the first time to General George Crook, thought by historians to be a fair, if somewhat harsh man, for his time. Upon taking office as the head of the Military Department in 1882, General Crook placed the blame for the Indian situation where it really belonged. "Greed and avarice on the part of the Whites, in other words the almighty dollar, is at the bottom of nine-tenths of our Indian problems." Geronimo, even though this first peace with the white man lasted only three years, wanted to bring an end to the conflicts with the white man.

In meeting General Crook the first time, Geronimo told Crook that he felt the Apache could fight indefinitely against the Mexicans, killing them by using rocks instead of rifles if need be, a chore that was not unpleasant to Geronimo, who had lost two wives and four children to the Spanish by the 1850's.

Geronimo in 1886.

But, Geronimo explained to General Crook, once the Gray Fox (Crook) came, guided by his own people (Apache from other tribes), he knew that he must either make terms or die fighting.

General Crook made peace with Geronimo and accepted his surrender while granting favorable terms to the Apache. Unfortunately for all parties, General Crook's terms were soon overridden in Washington and Geronimo, once again betrayed by the white man, was soon back on the warpath.

In 1881, Geronimo and his band were once again raiding with a band of 35 warriors, eight boys, and a hundred women and children. Geronimo and his band killed seventy-five civilians, twelve Indians of other tribes, two officers, eight soldiers and more than 100 Mexicans. Geronimo was wounded many times and lost six of his men, two boys, a woman and a child. The campaign was made possible by guerrilla warfare with Geronimo and his people striking in lightning fast raids, then retreating to hide in their mountain strongholds.

By 1886, the United States had five thousand troops pursuing the last of the Apache bands, and on September 4, 1886, Geronimo, the last of the Apache leaders to be apprehended, surrendered his band to General Crook for the second and final time, thus ending the Apache wars.

General Crook offered Geronimo and his people terms of two years in confinement, to be served outside the territory, after which they would be allowed to return to the reservation, rejoin their families, where they would be free. But once again, forces in Washington were not inclined to treat the Apache with honor. General Sheridan, with his typical disregard for promises made to Indians, insisted on an unconditional surrender, and the permanent imprisonment of the Apache band.

General Crook replied that he could not go back on his word to Geronimo and quickly resigned his command. Geronimo was confined to a prison in Florida until 1894, when his band was moved to the reservation at Fort Sill, Oklahoma, where he remained until his death on February 17, 1909.

same training as boys and practiced daily with bows and arrows, slings, and spears. They were taught horseback riding and combat. In times of war, wives were permitted to go on the warpath with their husbands.

Contrary to popular belief, the Apache did not scalp their victims. In fact, scalping was first introduced to the Southwestern Indians by the Spaniards. During the 1830's, Spaniards instituted a scalp-bounty system, an ancient Spanish practice, in which anyone bringing in the scalp of an adult male would be paid $100, an adult female paid $50 and $25 was paid for the scalp of a child.

This practice backfired in many ways. It was impossible to differentiate between an Apache scalp and those of other Indian tribes. Soon even friendly tribes were on the warpath as unscrupulous bounty hunters collected scalps wherever they could. Examining committees found it difficult to differentiate between the hair of Indians and Mexicans, and soon entire Mexican villages were murdered by bounty hunters to collect their grisly rewards. By 1837, the scalp-bounty system had escalated to unbelievable acts of violence and depravity.

James Johnson, a bounty hunter, illustrated the extent these despicable murderers would go to in their quest for profit. Johnson entered the Apache village of Juan Jose, where he was well known, with gifts for the Apache. Inside one sack was a small loaded cannon with its barrel tightly plugged. The Apaches gathered to see the "magic" Johnson had promised. Johnson lit the cannon's fuse with a cigar and calmly walked away, telling the Apache to keep watching the fuse. The cannon exploded, killing, or injuring, most of the Indians. Johnson and his men then calmly scalped the dead.

When an Apache was killed it obligated their relatives to seek revenge. Most large war parties were formed to avenge deaths. The Apache god Usen, the Supreme Being described by Geronimo and Cochise as creator and ruler of all things, had not commanded the Apache to forgive their enemies. Nor was one life considered enough for any Apache killed, often many lives were required to avenge the death of an Apache.

Apache chief Cochise once stated, "Americans began the fight, and now Americans and Mexicans kill an Apache on sight. I have retaliated with all my might. I have killed ten white men for every Indian slain."

Above: Big Bend National Park, Texas. The Comanche and Apache Indians frequented the area in raids on white settlers. Several forts were constructed nearby and utilized until peace treaties were finally signed in the late 1880's. PHOTO BY CARR CLIFTON

Continual harassment and encroachment by Spaniards in Apache territory, conflicts with the Comanche, Mexican domination, American occupation of Apache ancestral lands and increasing pressures and controls placed on the Apache, proved more than they could accept. A fragile coexistence with foreigners was abruptly brought to an end.

The great chiefs of the 1800's, Geronimo, Cochise, Mangus Coloradas, Nana, Loco and Victorio led their bands in raids and warfare against the white intruders. With the Apache, raiding had always been a way of life, with the primary objective of gathering horses, cattle, food and clothing. In warfare, fighting was the main objective, although Apaches always collected plunder after a battle.

Although there were countless skirmishes with the Apache during the mid to late 1800's, the final analysis found the Apache greatly overwhelmed by superior equipment, greater numbers and the use of their Indian brothers against them as scouts.

The Comanches began their rise to power in the Southwest around 1700. Increased mobility, provided by horses that had been introduced by the Spanish, extended the Comanche's range far beyond their traditional Wyoming region. They were horsemen without equal. Unlike other Indian tribes who would ride into battle and dismount to fight, Comanches fought their campaigns mounted. They were quick to capture the livestock of those they vanquished and owned vast herds of horses. It was not uncommon for a warrior to have more than 100 horses. Raiding parties traveled as far as Mexico and would return with as

QUANAH PARKER, COMANCHE WARLORD

The war between the Comanches and the American settlers began shortly after Texas won independence from Mexico. Ironically, the first major confrontation set the stage for the rise of the last of the great Comanche war chiefs. A raid on Parker's Fort, in east-central Texas, resulted in the capture of five white women and children, including nine-year old Cynthia Ann Parker.

Cynthia Ann adjusted well to Indian life. At eighteen, she married Chief Peta Nocona. She gave birth to Quanah, who became chief of the last Comanche band to surrender, as well as another son, and a daughter. Cynthia Ann was content with her life. In the 1850's, white buffalo hunters encountered her on the plains and offered to pay a ransom for her freedom. She refused, saying she had children to take care of and that she loved her husband.

When Quanah was fifteen, a raid by Texas Rangers and the U.S. Cavalry resulted in the recapture of Cynthia Ann Parker. As soldiers moved toward Cynthia Ann, thinking she was a man with her short hair and buffalo robe, she held her baby up, showing that she was a woman. Closer examination revealed her blue eyes, a trait not found in Indians. Convinced she was Cynthia Ann Parker, even though she spoke little English, the soldiers summoned her uncle, Isaac Parker, to aid in identifying her. As he was about to give up, feeling she was not his niece, he said: "Poor Cynthia Ann," to his surprise she replied: "Me Cynthia Ann."

She returned to her people, but was never again known to smile. On several occasions, she stole horses and set out in search of her

Comanche Chief Quanah, the son of Cynthia Ann Parker, a white woman captured by Comanches.

sons and husband. After four years with her relatives, her young daughter died of a fever. Cynthia Ann, devastated by the loss of the last of her family, starved herself to death.

Quanah became the greatest Comanche war chief, a legend in his time. In 1875, Quanah and his band became the last Comanches to surrender to reservation life. Quanah proved to be as great a leader in peace as in war, fighting for the Indians' rights, and making astute business deals with the whites that benefitted his tribe. The U.S. Congress praised his efforts. He lived for awhile with his mother's family, who gladly accepted him and taught him the white's ways.

many as 1,000 captured horses. By the middle of the 18th century they were well established on the southern plains, playing an important role in blocking northward expansion by the Spaniards, who were successfully contained in southern Texas. The Spaniards grew so weary of the continual raiding by Comanches, they enlisted the aid of the Apaches to attempt to drive them from Texas. The Spanish and Apache combined forces were defeated, with the Spanish driven to seek shelter in central Texas and the Apaches routed from the area.

Early in the 19th century, the Comanches occupied about 240,000 square miles of Texas, Colorado, Kansas, New Mexico and Oklahoma. The Spaniards, Apaches and Mexicans had proven unable to counteract the Comanche menace. In 1835, the Texans established the Texas Rangers, a small but incredibly tough militia. The Rangers fought the Comanche on their own terms, striking in raids when the Comanche least expected them, and began to turn the tide against Comanche domination of the region. As more Anglo-Americans began crossing Comanche territory on their way to the California gold fields in 1849, the Comanche were dealt their most serious blow by white intruders. This did not come from the forts built by the U.S. Army following the Mexican War of 1846, but from a cholera epidemic introduced by white prospectors. Comanches, who once numbered as many as 20,000, were decimated by the white man's disease, which killed about half of their population. Comanche forces never fully recovered from the epidemic.

In the 1860's, Quanah Parker, the last of the great Comanche war chiefs, preyed on white settlers on the plains of Texas. The son of a white woman, Cynthia Ann Parker, who was captured by Comanches as a young girl, and a Comanche chief, Quanah's daring raids and close escapes from the U. S. Cavalry rekindled war fever among the Plains Indians who still remained free from reservation existences. Quanah was the most feared of all Comanche chiefs, and the most fearless. Peace did not come to the region until his surrender in 1875. His was the last Comanche band to surrender. Quanah Parker proved himself to be a great leader in times of peace as well as times of war. He became a politician and financier who found ways to merge the interests of both the white men and his people. He searched for his mother, discovered her long dead, and then found solace living with her relatives who taught him to read and write English and the ways of the white man's world.

Right: A water sculpted pool in Wild Horse Canyon, near the base of the Rincon Mountains, in Saguaro National Monument. Tohono O'odham (Papago) Indians relied on the streams and wild foods of the area. Saguaro fruit is still used by the Tohono O'odham to make jam and a ceremonial wine.
PHOTO BY JACK W. DYKINGA

The Ute Indians of Colorado and the Paiutes of southern Utah are both related to Indians of the Great Basin tradition. The Utes, thought to be descendants of the Fremont culture, are historically the longest reigning residents of the state. They were the largest tribe and occupied a majority of the state's land. The Utes are the only tribe to hold reservations within the state's borders. Hunters and gatherers, the Utes did little farming and led a semi-nomadic existence.

The Utes are related to Paiutes, Comanches, Shoshones, and the Bannocks. Each of these tribes speak a Shoshonean language. They were known to trade with, and at times to raid, the Pueblos to the south and joined with their Comanche relatives to drive the Apache from the Colorado plains in the 18th century. Later, they formed a close association with the Jicarilla Apache, intermarrying and standing together against common enemies.

The Utes had no conflicts with the Spanish, and often allied with them against Comanches and Navajos. When the Americans first entered their territory, the Utes were unthreatened. By the mid 1800's, encroachment by settlers, and

Above: The Paiute Indians populated the Bryce Canyon National Park area, attaching spiritual values to its features. They occasionally used the canyon area for hunting and gathering.
PHOTO BY DICK DIETRICH

the presence of the U.S. Army, drove the Utes and their Jicarilla Apache allies to attack forts and settlements. This, in turn, led to reprisals by the military and the Utes sought peace. The last wild buffalo were gone, killed in 1897 in Lost Park, Colorado. The miners of the Pike's Peak Gold Rush swarmed the region, and the Utes moved to reservations, where the boundaries frequently changed as the white men coveted their land and broke promise after promise.

INDIAN ARTS AND CRAFTS

The Indians of the Southwest are known around the world for the quality of their arts and crafts. Traditional forms of pottery, basketry, jewelry and woven crafts remain extremely popular and are sought after by collectors. Today, many Indian artists are evolving the traditional designs in new and exciting directions. Whether traditional in design, or new in concept, the art and high quality crafts of Southwestern Indians are an important and exciting part of the international art world.

The Indians of the Southwest are known throughout the world for the quality of their unique arts and crafts. The pottery, basketry, jewelry, and woven goods created by Native American craftsmen contribute substantially to both the art world and the economies of the Southwestern tribes each year. Although most people are familiar with traditional crafts and designs, today a new generation of artisans is emerging among the Southwestern Indian tribes. They are more contemporary than their ancestors and are gaining considerable fame and admiration in the field of Indian arts and crafts, and in the art world in general.

The Hopi Indians are accomplished artisans and craftsmen. Well known for their exquisite carvings of kachinas, watercolor paintings, basketry, pottery and silverwork, the Hopi derive considerable income from the sale of their arts and crafts.

Hopi pottery is extremely well crafted and shows the strong influence of their roots in Anasazi and Mogollon cultures. The majority of Hopi pottery is produced on First Mesa.

Hopi silverwork designs have been evolving since the later part of the nineteenth century, but were originally inspired by contact with Zuñi and Navajo silversmiths. A Zuñi silversmith named Layande was responsible for training the first Hopi silversmith, Sikyatala, in the art of silver working in the late 1880's.

The fine quality of Hopi overlay jewelry stands on its own merits and is especially popular. Their overlay designs are sometimes fashioned after Hopi pottery and basketry designs, incorporating a wide variety of stylized elements, including some very popular animal motifs. Silverwork designs often include inlay work of turquoise and coral.

The use of silver has been a relatively new part of Hopi jewelry making. During the early 1900's, silver was extremely hard for Hopi craftsmen to obtain. Sometimes when they would run out of the precious metal, they would ride or walk to Winslow, Arizona, where they would "acquire" silverware from local restaurants. They would then take the silverware to the nearest railroad track, place it on the rails, and wait for the trains to compress the silver into a pliable material. Today, Hopi craftsmen are not faced with shortages of raw materials. Their fine designs and excellent craftsmanship have become quite successful in the marketplace, so Hopi jewelry makers of today use only the finest materials in the creation of their art.

The Hopi art of kachina, or katsina, making has its roots in the ceremonial kivas and the religion of the Hopi people and their Anasazi (Hisatsinom) ancestors. Kachina are believed to be supernatural beings who dwell in the mountains, lakes, and springs and bestow blessings on the Pueblo people. They are the spirits dwelling in all things. Most kachinas are benevolent in nature and are responsible for rain, successful crops, and good health; others are ogres, or demons, and represent disciplinary functions. Hopi legends tell of the kachina bringing gifts and teaching the Indians arts and crafts. The kachina taught some of the faithful their ceremonies, how to

Left: Blue A'hote kachina carving (17" tall) by Edward Tewanema, Hopi.
PHOTO BY JERRY JACKA
Courtesy McGees Beyond Native Tradition Gallery, Holbrook.AZ

Right: Navajo squash blossom necklace in center by Leonard Benally. Clockwise from top: silver box by Tommy Curtis, Navajo; Navajo bracelet by Jerry Begay; Zuni bracelet, signed TAH; Zuni pin with dangles by Irma Octavius; round Zuni pin, and pin with coral, both unsigned; Zuni cluster pin by Alice Quam; Zuni cluster bracelet, signed LMB.
PHOTO BY JERRY JACKA
Courtesy The Heard Museum Gift Shop, Phoenix, Arizona

make masks and costumes, and permitted them, as long as they were pure of heart, to act as if they were kachinas. If the ceremonies were enacted properly, the real kachinas would come and possess the masked dancers.

The kachinas are represented in various ways, all interconnected in the Pueblo peoples' minds. First, they are considered to be human, although they are not from this world. They are also the masked, costumed and painted dancers who appear in kivas and village plazas as impersonators of the spiritual kachinas to perform rites and ceremonies, which are artforms in themselves. Lastly, they are also the wooden figurines, small carved images of the life-sized beings, and they are revered by all the Pueblo people. The children use the figurines to study the ways of the kachina, and adults collect them in much the same manner Christians collect images of Christ on the Cross or statues of the Virgin Mary and their many saints. The incredible beauty and surrealistic properties of kachina carvings make them extremely popular with non-Indian art collectors as well.

The Navajo are an Athabascan people who migrated to the Southwest region from Canada more than 1,000 years ago. They were nomadic hunters and gatherers, and were not inclined to live in close knit villages like the Hopi and

Above: Modern Zuñi Indian Fetishes. Pueblo Indians of the Southwest believe fetishes contain spirits with the ability to give their owner supernatural powers.
PHOTO BY JERRY JACKA   Art Courtesy of Godbers Gifts, Phoenix, Arizona

Pueblo Indians of the Southwest. An intelligent and creative people, the Navajo were quick to learn the arts and crafts of the Pueblo Indians they encountered. Early Navajo weavings were primarily of cotton and natural fibers. Given the fragile nature of these fibers, little now remains of early Navajo woven crafts.

Even though hostile clashes between the Navajo and Pueblos were not uncommon, given the fierce raiding nature of the early Navajo, it was the Rio Grande Pueblo Indians

who taught the Navajo how to weave the beautiful wool rugs that they are now famous for worldwide. After the Pueblo Revolt of 1680, many Rio Grande area Pueblo Indians fled west to the lands of the Hopi and Navajo to escape retaliation from the Spaniards.

Weaving in wool did not begin in the Southwest until sheep were introduced by the Spaniards about A.D. 1600. The oldest examples of Navajo weaving ever found were discovered in Massacre Cave in Canyon del Muerto, at Canyon de Chelly National Monument on the Navajo Reservation. They were found, in 1805, as the Spaniards inspected the cave after they had killed around 100 Navajo warriors, women and children.

Navajo arts of jewelry making and metal work are synonymous with silver and turquoise. The turquoise stone is believed, by Navajo and many other groups of people around the world, to possess benign powers that ward off calamities and many of life's hazards. Although metal work by the Navajo dates from the middle of the 19th century, all early work was done in iron or copper. The Navajo men learned the art of metal working when they were detained at Fort Sumner, after the "Long Walk" that marked the end of the Navajo's freedom to live as they pleased and incarcerated them at the Bosque Redondo

THE KACHINA

The kachina, or katsina, are believed by the Pueblo Indians to be supernatural beings who dwell in mountains, lakes, and springs and bestow many blessings on the Pueblo people. Kachina are the spirits of all things, from the birds in the sky to the corn in the fields. Among the Zuñi people they are known as koko.

Most kachina are benevolent in nature and are responsible for rain, successful crops, and good health. Other kachinas are ogres, or demons, and are used to represent disciplinary functions. It is said that ogres will eat children who do not obey the kachinas, or do not behave themselves.

Kachinas, according to Pueblo legends, were real beings and would visit the Pueblo people when they were sad, or lonely, and would dance for them. The kachina brought gifts and taught the Indians arts and crafts, how to build their villages, cultivate their crops, and to hunt. As time went by, the Pueblo people began to take the kachina for granted and lost respect for their benevolence. Violent struggles broke out between the Pueblo Indians and the supernatural beings. Finally, the kachina quit visiting the Pueblos.

Because the kachina truly cared for the Pueblo people, they taught some of the faithful their ceremonies, how to make kachina masks and costumes, and permitted them, as long as they were pure of heart, to act as if they were kachinas. If the kachina ceremony was enacted properly, real kachinas would then appear and take possession of the masked dancers.

Although all members of the Pueblo tribes are initiated into the Kachina Society, only men are allowed to impersonate the kachinas.

Kachinas are represented in various ways, all connected in the minds of the Pueblo people. First, they are considered to be human, although they are not; they are the masked, costumed and painted dancers who appear in kivas and village plazas as impersonators of the spiritual kachinas to perform rites and ceremonies; and they are the wooden figurines, small carved images of the life-sized beings, revered by all the Pueblo

Above: Hopi kachina dolls. From left to right: Mountain Sheep by Myron Gaseona; Lizard by D. Polingyumptewa; Ogre by Eddie Torivio, Sr.; Kokosori by Cecil Calnimptewa.
PHOTO BY JERRY JACKA   Art Courtesy of McGee's Beyond Native Tradition Gallery, Holbrook, Arizona

people. Children use the figurines to study the ways of the kachina, and adults collect them in the same manner Christians collect images of Christ or statues of the Virgin Mary.

reservation in New Mexico. No silver work was fashioned until the Navajo returned to their homelands, the site of the present day Navajo Reservation that occupies portions of northern Arizona, northwestern New Mexico and southeastern Utah.

Early production methods were crude and inefficient, but the quality and production of silver jewelry gradually increased. It was not until around 1880 that settings of any kind

Above: Finely crafted silver overlay jewelry set with coral, by Hopi jeweler Phil Poseyesva.
PHOTO BY JERRY JACKA
Art Courtesy of Waddell Trading Co., Tempe, Arizona

were made, and bits of glass, beads and garnets were introduced in Navajo silverwork designs. Around 1900, turquoise began to appear in increasing quantities and thereafter became closely associated with the Navajo silverwork designs.

A wide range of silver articles are currently produced by the Navajo: conchas for belts, buttons, rings, earrings, bracelets, necklaces, hat bands and more. The influence of other tribes and cultures can be seen in the Navajo work. Conchas strung on belts were inspired by the silver disks that hung from the belts of Plains Indian women. The most common type of necklace is made of large, hollow, silver beads that are separated by flower shaped pendants. These are commonly called "squash blossom" necklaces because of the pendant feature. The squash blossom design copied the

Right: Mosaic and inlay jewelry styles. The silver pendant, signed Booqua, and the necklace, which is unsigned, are made by the Zuñi. The earrings, by Joe Cote, and shell pendant, by Mary Lovato, are Santo Domingo.
PHOTO BY JERRY JACKA
Art Courtesy of The Heard Museum Gift Shop, Phoenix, Arizona

pomegranate blossoms used to adorn Spanish clothing and saddlery, but these designs are now considered to be traditional Navajo Indian jewelry designs.

The Zuñi are accomplished silver workers. In addition, they craft the majority of fetishes used by Southwestern Indians. Fetishes are objects in which it is believed spirits live, and are thought to have the ability to give their owners supernatural powers. Use of fetishes dates to prehistoric times. Ownership of fetishes is held by individuals, clans, societies or kivas.

The most prized fetishes by the Indians are those that are naturally formed and shaped like animals. These items may be of stone, shell, antler or other materials. Fetishes that are carved by Zuñi fetish makers are highly respected by other tribes. These are often adorned with small bits of shell, turquoise and coral, which is thought to increase their powers.

Although they were once accomplished in all forms of arts and crafts, silver jewelry represents the great majority of Zuñi crafts produced today. Basketry and weaving are rarely practiced, and pottery is produced on a diminished scale, as are kachinas.

Pueblo Indians, and their ancestors, in the Southwest have been producing pottery for nearly two thousand years. The earliest pots were utility wares that served to increase the quality of life by providing better storage and

Above: Jewelry by Perry Shorty, Navajo. The concha belt, necklace and pin were awarded first place ribbons at the 1991 Arts & Crafts Expo during the Navajo Nation Fair at Window Rock, Arizona.
PHOTO BY JERRY JACKA   Art Courtesy of Hubbell Trading Post, Ganado, Arizona

cooking abilities than baskets. As the shapes, styles and techniques used in pottery making evolved, it was not long before Indian women began to decorate their wares, and individuals within the same group often used the same designs. Although work of a single craftsman can sometimes be found and identified among items in prehistoric finds, it was not until earlier this century that Pueblo Indians began to sign their pottery, signifying a change to individual styles.

In addition to the fine pottery produced by the Hopi, excellent pottery is produced by many other Pueblo Indians. Acoma produces fine traditional pottery, in addition to creations that blend traditional designs with exciting

new techniques and materials. At Zia Pueblo, traditional pottery making is still practiced, with distinctive designs in red clay and mineral black that often feature a bird motif. Jemez and Santo Domingo Pueblos also produce pottery with traditional designs.

In 1895, Lesou, a Hopi Indian from Hano on First Mesa, who was a member of the Jesse Fewkes Expedition of the same year, brought his wife, Nampeyo, pieces of prehistoric Hopi pottery found at Sikatki and Awatovi. Nampeyo incorporated these ancient designs into her pottery and to this day their descendants have carried on this style, with all their work being known as Nampeyo Hopi pottery. Work by Joy Navasie features a white slip decorated with natural mineral red and black designs that have become extremely popular. This style originated with Joy's mother, Frog Woman (Paqua), and is carried on by Joy's daughters.

At San Ildefonso and San Carlos Pueblos, pottery designs have become decidedly more contemporary during this century. At San Ildefonso Pueblo, highly polished red and black wares with matte designs, and carved wares have long been popular. The work of Blue Corn has developed into several styles that meld traditional designs with a contemporary style that often incorporates backgrounds of white, red and orange.

Santa Clara Pueblo pottery is similar in design to San Ildefonso styles and is often decorated with animal and bird figures. Several exceptional potters, producing highly collectable art, are found at Santa Clara. Laguna Pueblo produces pottery that is similar to Acoma, but normally with heavier walls and art that is not as carefully executed. The Acoma

Above: Hopi pottery. Clockwise from upper left: polychrome jar by Maynard and Veronica Navasie; carved seed bowl by E. Hamilton; large jar by Ravin Nampeyo; two jars by Neva P. Nampeyo; black on white seed bowl by Burel Naha; small carved jar by Iris Nampeyo.
PHOTO BY JERRY JACKA
Art Courtesy of The Heard Museum Gift Shop, Phoenix, Arizona

Pueblo pottery has the thinnest walls and lightest weights of modern Pueblo Indian pottery. The Cochiti Pueblo is famous for pottery that often is shaped in the form of birds, and for their humorous figures styled to represent people and animals.

Pottery is still being produced by non-Pueblo Indians, including the Tohono O'otam (Papago), Navajo, Maricopa and others, but are generally utility ware that are not highly decorated.

Basket making pre-dates the invention of pottery in the Southwest. The earliest Indians used woven baskets to gather and store foods. A variety of designs were made, including baskets that were lined with a coating of pitch which made them water-tight for cooking foods. Cooking with baskets was generally accomplished by placing heated stones inside baskets that contained food. Although this resulted in a great number of baskets being burned, it was a better process than warming some items directly over a flame.

Among most tribes of the Southwest, basket making is slowly disappearing as a viable commercial endeavor. Countless hours needed to create tightly woven baskets are rarely rewarded financially. The Tohono O'otam produce more baskets than any other tribe in the U.S. Baskets are used in a number of Indian ceremonies by Hopi, Navajo, Apache and other tribes. Baskets are still in demand by some

Above: Coiled baskets and raw materials by Elene Atokuku, Hopi. At left is a kachina design of crow mother; at right is a Qögöli kachina design.
PHOTO BY JERRY JACKA
Courtesy of Tsakurshovi, Second Mesa, Arizona

Left: Pueblo Indian pottery of the Southwest. Far left: vase by Sunbird of Santa Clara Pueblo; upper left: jar by Noreen Simplicio, Zuñi; far right: jar by Alvina Yeppa, Jemez Pueblo; left front: seed jar by Sondra Victorino, Acoma Pueblo; center: vase by S. Lewis, Acoma Pueblo; right front: miniature jar by W. Aragon of Acoma Pueblo.
PHOTO BY JERRY JACKA
Art Courtesy of The Heard Museum Gift Shop, Phoenix, Arizona

tribes that have now ceased making their own baskets, even though they are no longer quite as popular with many non-Indian buyers as they once were.

The Hopi of Arizona still produce tightly woven coiled baskets, bowls, plaques and containers that are quite beautiful. They also produce plaited yucca sifter baskets on all three of their mesas.

The Apache, although once famous for fine basketry, now produce only a more utilitarian ware. Several other Southwestern tribes produce a limited number of baskets, most of which are relatively plain in design.

Seri Indians, of northwest Mexico along the Sea of Cortez, produce good quality coiled baskets that are often found in stores throughout the Southwest. The import items are popular with both Native

Above: A group of coiled baskets. Top row (left to right): Papago, 10" tall; Hopi plaque, 16" diameter; Hopi container, 12" diameter. Center row (left to right): Seri olla by Panchita Moreno, 8" tall with a 10" diameter; Seri shallow bowl by Aurolia Molina, 13" diameter; Navajo wedding basket, 12" diameter. Front: Papago miniature horsehair baskets by Dorena and Ruby Garcia.
PHOTO BY JERRY JACKA

American tribes and with non-Indian buyers. The region the Seri occupy is actually similar in

all ways to the Southwestern United States and, but for the international boundary, would be considered a region of the Southwest. The Seri are perhaps most famous for their carved ironwood figures, which they only began producing during the 1960's. The Seri had been fishermen until Mexican shrimp boats destroyed Seri fishing areas. Seri carvers had long been using ironwood to make different types of tools, musical instruments, bowls, kitchen utensils and other items. Without their fishing grounds to provide income and sustenance for the tribe, the Seri began to carve ironwood figures of birds, fish, and animals, carvings that were immediately popular with visitors to their area. During the late 1960's, Seri art began to be exported to the United States.

NAVAJO RUG WEAVING

The Navajo learned the art of weaving from Pueblo Indians fleeing the Rio Grande Valley, in New Mexico, after the Pueblo Revolt of 1680. The Pueblo Indians are thought to have either joined the Navajo to escape possible retribution from the Spaniards, or possibly were captured by the Navajos in their flight to safety.

The Navajo acquired sheep from early Spanish colonists and were adept herdsmen, their semi-nomadic lifestyle being perfectly suited to raising sheep and cattle. During the early years of Navajo weaving, designs primarily were copied from those of their Pueblo teachers. They were simple in concept and in their use of color. Most were comprised of stripes in natural sheep colors; black, brown, white and gray. Grays were achieved by the carding of black and white wools together. The early Navajo woven goods were mainly dresses and blankets.

The Navajo have always been a bright and creative people and soon began to elaborate on the designs of their Pueblo teachers. Geometric designs were introduced and the range of colors amplified by the use of vegetal dyes, indigo blue dye, introduced by the Spaniards, and cochineal red cloth the Spaniards supplied that the Navajo unraveled and respun into yarn. During the 1700's and 1800's, Navajo blankets were widely respected for their quality and were a sought after trade product by the Indian, Spanish and Anglo-American traders.

During the late 1880's, the market for Navajo blankets became saturated as cheaper, softer

Left: A Ganado Red Navajo weaving by Rena Yazzie featuring a Teec Nos Pos design.
PHOTO BY JERRY JACKA
Courtesy of Margaret Kilgore Gallery, Scottsdale, Arizona

Above: Double rug by Sarah Begay. Inside is a Yei design Burnt Water, outside is Crystal. This rug won first place as the Most Innovative in the Navajo Show 1987, Museum of Northern Arizona, Flagstaff.
PHOTO BY JERRY JACKA

blankets produced by woolen mills replaced the demand for hand woven Navajo products. Traders then demanded thicker woven products, often with borders to frame Navajo designs, that could be used for rugs.

Navajo designs are named for the area in which they are produced. Two Grey Hills, Lukachukai, Three Turkey Ruin, Crystal, Black Mountain, Teec Nos Pos and Ganado areas each produce designs distinct in colors and pattern. In the Shiprock area, sand painting designs are incorporated in rugs. These designs, considered sacred, are altered to allow their use for commercial purposes, and comprise the Yei and Yeibechai rug designs.

SOUTHWESTERN POINTS OF INTEREST...

ARIZONA'S POINTS OF INTEREST

Bisbee...1880's copper mining town. **Canyon de Chelly National Monument**...Anasazi ruins. **Casa Grande Ruins National Monument**...Ruins of the Hohokam culture. **Chiricahua National Monument**...Chiricahua Apache homeland and site of Faraway Ranch. **Colossal Cave**...Natural limestone cave near Tucson. **Coronado National Memorial**...Commemorates Coronado's expedition into the U.S. **Desert Botanical Gardens**...Located in Phoenix. Desert plants in natural surroundings. **Fort Bowie National Historic Site**...Ruins of fort used in operations against Geronimo and Cochise. **Fort Huachuca**... Historic fort and museum. **Fort Verde State Park**...Fort from 1870's Indian Wars. **Glen Canyon National Recreation Area**...Includes Glen Canyon Dam. **Grand Canyon National Park**...One of the Seven Natural Wonders of the World. **Heard Museum**...Located in Phoenix. Excellent examples of Southwestern Indian arts and crafts. **Heritage Square**...Restored turn of the century buildings in Phoenix. **Hubbell Trading Post National Historic Site**...100 year old Indian trading post on the Navajo Reservation. **Jerome**...Historical mining town, museum and historical displays. **Lake Mead National Recreational Area**...Created by Hoover Dam. **Meteor Crater**...Site of the impact of a giant meteor. **Mission San Xavier del Bac**...Spanish mission established in 1700. **Montezuma Castle National Monument**...Sinagua culture ruins. **Museum of Northern Arizona**...In Flagstaff. Displays natural history and history of northern Arizona, Indian arts and crafts. **Navajo National Monument**...Anasazi ruins of Betatakin, Keet Seel and Inscription House. **Organ Pipe Cactus Natl. Monument**...Plants and animals of the Sonoran Desert. **Petrified Forest National Park**...Petrified trees, Anasazi ruins, and remains of Triassic-age animals. **Pioneer Arizona Museum**...North of Phoenix. History of 1880's Arizona. **Pipe Spring National Monument**...Fort built by pioneers in 1870's. **Prescott Territorial Capital**...Historic mining town and site of Arizona's first capital. **Pueblo Grande**...Hohokam ruins in Phoenix. **Saguaro National Monument**...Preserves cactus unique to the Sonoran desert. **Sonoran Desert Museum**...Desert flora and fauna in Tucson. **Sunset Crater Volcano National Monument**...Volcanic cinder cone from eruption in A.D. 1065. **Tombstone**...Famous old west silver mining town. **Tonto National Monument**...Salado cliff dwellings. **Tumacacori National Historical Park**...Historic Spanish mission. **Tuzigoot National Monument**...Sinagua ruins. **Walnut Canyon National Monument**...Sinagua cliff dwellings. **Wupatki National Monument**...Sinagua culture pueblos and archeological sites. **Yuma Territorial Prison**...Housed criminals during territorial days.

Right: Great Sand Dunes National Monument in southern Colorado is the site of the largest sand dunes found in North America. Explorer John C. Fremont explored this region in the late 1840's.
PHOTO BY JACK W. DYKINGA

COLORADO'S POINTS OF INTEREST

Bent's Old Fort National Historic Site... Fort and trading center on Santa Fe Trail. **Durango**...Historic mining supply center. **Durango and Silverton Narrow Gauge Railroad**...Authentic steam powered train from Durango to Silverton. **Great Sand Dunes National Monument**...Tallest sand dunes found in U.S. **Hovenweep National Monument**...Anasazi ruins. **Mesa Verde National Park**...Pueblos, pithouses and cliff dwellings of the Anasazi. **Silverton**...Historic Victorian silver and gold mining town. **Telluride**...Late 1800's gold mining town. **Yucca House National Monument**...Indian pueblo west of Mesa Verde.

NEW MEXICO'S POINTS OF INTEREST

Aztec Ruins National Monument...Ruins of the Anasazi Indian culture. **Bandelier National Monument**...Anasazi Ruins. **Capulin Volcano National Monument**...Remains of volcanic cinder cone. **Carlsbad Caverns National Park**...Underground caverns and unusual formations. **Chaco Culture National Historical Park**...Ruins of Anasazi culture. **El Malpais Natl. Monument**...Remnants of 30 volcanoes. **El Morro National Monument**...Sandstone bluff with "Inscription Rock" signed by prehistoric Indians, early Spanish and American explorers. **Fort Union National Monument**...Ruins of U.S. Army fort. **Gila Cliff Dwellings National Monument**...Ruins of the Mogollon culture. **Pecos National Historical Park**...Ruins of Pecos Pueblo and two Spanish colonial missions. **Salinas Pueblo Missions National Monument**...Ruins of Indian pueblos and three Spanish missions. **Santa Fe**...City rich in Spanish and Indian art and culture. **Taos**...Picturesque art colony, home of Taos Indian Pueblo, historic homes including Kit Carson's. **Zuni-Cibola National Historical Park**...Zuni cultural and historical sites.

TEXAS' POINTS OF INTEREST

The Alamo...Mission used in Texans' fight for independence. **Alibates Flint Quarries National Monument**...Prehistoric Indian tool making site. **Big Bend National Park**...Natural area and World Biosphere Reserve. **Chamizal National Memorial**...Commemorates history of U.S. border with Mexico. **Fort Davis National Historic Site**...Fort used in Indian Wars. **Guadalupe Mountains National Park**...Natural area. **Lake Meredith National Recreation Area**...Water sports. **Padre Island National Seashore**...Gulf Coast beaches. **Palo Alto Battlefield National Historic Site**...Commemorates site of Mexican War battle. **Rio Grande Wild and Scenic River**...Natural area. **San Antonio Missions National Historical Park**...Preserves four Spanish colonial missions.

UTAH'S POINTS OF INTEREST

Arches National Park...Unique erosional features. **Bryce Canyon National Park**...Erosion formed pinnacles, walls and amphitheaters. **Canyonlands National Park**...Natural formations and prehistoric Indian sites. **Capitol Reef National Park**... Sandstone formations along the Fremont River. **Cedar Breaks National Monument**...Large natural amphitheater. **Glen Canyon National Recreation Area**...Formed by Glen Canyon Dam. **Hovenweep National Monument**...Anasazi ruins. **Natural Bridges National Monument**...Natural bridges carved from sandstone. **Rainbow Bridge Natl. Monument**...World's largest natural bridge. **Zion National Park**...Scenic canyon and mesas.

Right: Cottonwoods changing to their fall colors in Utah's Zion National Park.
PHOTO BY JEFF GNASS

Outside Back Cover: Betatakin, Navajo for "ledge house," is an Anasazi cliff dwelling at Navajo National Monument in northern Arizona.
PHOTO BY TOM DANIELSEN